In the beginning, life was as simple as milk and cookies. And then...

conceived, written and produced
by
THOMAS HAGEY

Text edited by Elizabeth Rubin

Art direction by Kelvin Case, Dale Moser and Thomas Hagey

Design/Art for cover, inside/outside, fron/back plus pages nine through twenty-four (inclusive) by Barry and Linda Lavender, Let 'er Ring! Graphics

With thanks to Moveable Type, Steve, Bob and Mother Mary

PRODUCTION AND ASSEMBLY

The Art Works, Toronto — with special thanks to Ted Young, Brenda Siddall and Ken Hartley

PRODUCTION COORDINATION

Emmanuel Papadakis and David Liang

SEPARATIONS AND FILM

Aurora Colour Imaging, Mississauga

PHOTOGRAPHY

Studio photography by Steve Lawrence, in association with John James Wood Photography Studio, Toronto

Exterior photography by Steve Lawrence, Stan Switalski and Thomas Hagey

Cover photo by Stan Switalski

Centerfold photo by Steve Lawrence

Additional photography and assistance by Lisette Bourdages

Photo retouching by Bob Suzuki, Nancy Hum, Al Pease

Hand tinting of author's photo by Jody Hewgill

ILLUSTRATIONS

Clarence Porter, Kelvin Case, Robert Markle, Dale Moser and Ted Sivell

Covers and centerfold airbrushing by Bob Suzuki

Photo montage by Richard Slye

Clay sculptures by Ted Sivell

Paper sculpture by Ron Broda

Leather design by Brad Balch

FOOD STYLIST

Claire Stancer

TYPESETTING

Sherkid Creative Typography Inc.

Moveable Type

PROPS

The Art Works, Dale Moser, Kim Dewar, Deb Carson, Wendy Fulton, Barry Lavender, Noor Hogben, Winnie Mertens, John Hagey. Cookies by Linda Lavender.

Props supplied by: Ketchum Manufacturing Ltd., Guelph/Ottawa; Mannion's Furniture of Cambridge; Lorien Jewellers, Toronto; George's Trains, Toronto.

THANKS TO THE FOLLOWING FARMERS:

Don and Jean Albrecht, Tim and Wendy Beirnes, George Dalton, Neil and Janice McCaig, John and Dorothy Harkness, Charles Watson, Larry Sheardown and Rexlea Jerseys, Oakwald Farms Ltd., Speedside Holsteins, Mt. Elgin Dairy Farms, Shaver Poultry.

THANKS TO THE FOLLOWING:

Tracey Alexander, Bruce Ettinger, Marsha Boulton, Richard Cooper Betty Gallander, Wayne Oakley, Barbara Allen, Gary Shepherd, Frank Etherington, Glen Stemmler, K-W Record, CKCO-TV, Tom Lewis and Bev, Ron Gerston, Judy Bottomley, Stanley Peter Owens, Drew Miller, Harry Mathews, Rhonda Mathews, Danny McMulin, Corbin McMulin, Soren Jakobsen, Sandy Switalski, Brennan Hagey, John James Wood, Mike and Sue Wilgus, Bruce Anderson, Mongo, Tim, Al, Alice Williams, Marjorie Lewis, Ken McKay, Leslie, Barb, Art Plastics, Hazel

and Harold Roberts, Cheryl and Larry Van Daele, Ginny Berrill, Glen Kicksee, Margaret and Dennis Hewitt, Denise and Jamie Fisher, Helen Bridle, Russell Gammon, Peter Doswell, Mary E. Lea, Reid Bannister, Truckin' T-Shirts, Wendy Davis, Mark and Phyllis Silverstein, Peter Butler, Mel Davis, Bob Gentry, Mike Soro, Serge Trajkovich, Imperial Autobody, Lucinda Vardey Agency, Queen's Tavern-Ayr, Ken Tatimichi and Minolta Canada (Sometimes you get the bull and sometimes the bull gets you—unless you're using the 75-300 mm lense by Minolta. Then it's "Na! Na! Na! Na! Na! Na!". Thomas Hagey uses the Minolta 9000 Maxxum.).

SPECIAL THANKS TO:

Kent Heiden, Mary E. Lea, Harry Mathews, Wendy Fulton, Deb Carson, Steve Lawrence, Stan Switalski, my brother John, Elizabeth Rubin, all of my friends and, most of all, to the "Big Guy" for helping me get through.

Cowsmopolitan, written by Thomas Hagey and published by Firefly Books Ltd., is not licenced by or affiliated in any way with any existing magazine or publication. All names, products, addresses, phone numbers and identifying marks of any kind other than the information appearing on the masthead (page two) and the MOO JEANS ad on p. 64 are purely fictional. Any similarity to real persons, living or dead, firms, corporations or products is purely coincidental.

Cowsmopolitan is a trademark of Thomas Hagey.

Cataloguing in Publication Data

Hagey, Thomas.

Cowsmopolitan.

ISBN 1-55209-058-2

1. Cows – Humor.   2. Cosmopolitan (New York, N.Y.: 1952) – Parodies, imitations, etc. I. Title

PN6231.C24H34 1996   C818'.5407   C96-931399-3

Cowsmopolitan is dedicated to my family. To my parents, Lloyd and Bertha May, tor their support, both moral and financial. And my siblings, Rebecca, Mary and John, tor their support and for scaring the daylights out of me every time Mom and Dad went away ("Toooommy! There's a humanoid under your bed.")

With love from the "Little White Bird"

—Toronto, September 1987—

A FIREFLY BOOK

Published by Firefly Books Ltd. 1996

Firefly Books Ltd.
3680 Victoria Park Avenue
Willowdale, Ontario
Canada M2H 3K1

Published in the U.S. by
Firefly Books (U.S.) Inc.
P.O. Box 1338, Ellicott Station
Buffalo, New York 14205

Printed and bound in Canada

COWSMOPOLITAN

^{TM}

Cover Look

▲ *A Class Act*

Departments

Friction

Articles and Features

▼ *Forbidden Love*

Celebrities

Beauty and Fashion

Food and Wine and Decorating

▲ *Mr. Avail A. Bull*

Mr. Avail A. Bull *is* indeed a stud and lives with Don and Jean Albrecht

Clover Girl® creates new

Continuous Comment

At last! Luscious colors
that won't come off your lips
'cause they don't go on your lips.*

Clover Girl

Cheryl Teats isn't wearing anything at all

© 1987 Clover Girl

*Comes in handy, though. Ideal for floors, walls (including brick),
mirrors, or just keep it by the phone.

STOMP INTO MY PARLOR

Chicken

by Ellen Guernsey Brown

As Editor of this magazine, I feel that I have a moral responsibility to tell it like it is. Unfortunately, they don't give me the opportunity or the space. Another good idea from the pen of Ellen Guernsey Brown, Editor of Cowsmopolitan — out the window!

Far too often, I find myself on 2/3 of a page, sharing the rest of it with an ad. One month they put me across from a "feminine itching" ad. I put a stop to that. A fine way to treat a celebrity!

First off, my name is Ellen Guernsey Brown. I am the Editor of this magazine. I'm not sure if I told you this already, so I thought I'd tell you now — just in case I hadn't told you yet.

Many of you, no doubt, are curious how our magazine works. Let me fill you in. Our feature and contributing writers get to write features and contribute writing. My contribution (besides dropping a few names here and there — which never hurts) is to talk about their contributions. Their influence on each issue is substantial. Mine is, well . . . Hmmm? I wonder if I'm moody enough. Perhaps I'm too accessible to coworkers. Maybe they've begun to take me for granted. Or worse yet, "granite".

Is our problem here that we've got a good thing going and we don't want any boat-rocking? Is this healthy? Does this include me? I mean, I'm as much in favor of smooth sailing as the next cow, but surely the occasional swell or even ripple is healthy.

Is our formula for success so firmly in place that we can't deviate from it — not even for our readers' benefit? Is our advertisement-to-editorial ratio out of whack? Do we police the advertising enough? At all? ARE WE GREEDY? LOOKIT, IF WE ARE I WANT TO KNOW ABOUT IT! And why all the rhetorical questions all of a sudden?

Are our readers more neurotic after reading Cowsmo — or less neurotic? Would I hire Oliver North? Is that America's problem? Would we all hire Oliver North? Something tells me that many of us would. But not without Fawn, of course.

Why is sex such a big stumbling block for cows? Has so much emphasis been placed on performance that we can't relax with each other? Do bulls really want cows to howl like a banshee during lovemaking (be their Demon Love Goddess)? Or babble incoherent chatter (symbolizing something, perhaps a form of deep devotion, I can't be sure)? AND then, almost in the same breath (although slightly out of), ask to be read a bedtime story (be their Mother). Do bulls want a performance clause in the marriage contract _and_ a bedtime story, too? Is this fair?

Why is it that Colleen Hildenbrandt's udder seems to have been big forever? Explain to me why her udder was so much larger than everyone else's in the fifth grade when her mother wasn't exactly what I call "top heavy".

Why is it that mothers sit their daughters down when they reach puberty and, in so many words, tell them that something dreadful will be taking place soon — most likely this year. Of course, she couldn't give you all the details, but she did find the courage to say that "This alone will make you a woman."

No mention of how you might prepare yourself for the humiliation that was to follow (and follow it does) all the way through life. No quick tips. No crash course in how to howl like a banshee on command. Just a lot of bad news all at once with no answers. Whatever happened to the simplicity that accompanied the milk and cookies era, anyway?

And as a magazine which publishes articles of the above nature, are we addressing these problems or contributing to them?

And another thing: if I'm the driving force behind the editorial direction of this publication, if I'm its very pulse, its conscience — then why, all of a sudden, do I get the feeling that I'm about to interview a chicken? I don't think a "chicken interview" is going to do my image a heck of a lot of good. On the other hand, if it says on the front cover that I'm going to interview a chicken and I don't . . . Could it be a joke?

I think I had best call a meeting with the Art Director and the editorial committee immediately following this issue to find out how that chicken thing got on the cover to begin with. This is news to me.

Now, if you'll excuse me, I have to . . . well, ah . . . do this rather important interview. Crisis in the poultry industry — that sort of hard-hitting stuff which not everyone can do . . .

E.G.B.: I'M going to be interviewing YOU?

Chicken: Lookit! You're lucky you got a chicken to come here at all — this is our "busy" time.

E.G.B.: Well, you certainly are a Chicken, aren't you? Would you prefer if I used "Boc! Boc! Boc-ity Boc!"?

Chicken: You do that very well, but you don't have to talk like a Chicken for my sake. I _can_ speak English.

E.G.B.: Poulez vous Poulet? That means "Do you speak Chicken?" in French.

Chicken: Nice touch but not necessary. Parisians might be impressed — Chickens aren't. At least, not this one.

E.G.B.: Okay. Straight to the good stuff. It must have been a great honor to have won the Pulitzer Prize for your writing. How did you react when you were first notified?

Chicken: Wrong Chicken! I've never won a Pulitzer Prize. Now . . . a Pullet Surprise . . . ? That's a different story. Actually, I've never won a Pullet Surprise myself, but I did hear of one being raffled off at a gentlemen's stag.

The groom, apparently, was holding the lucky ticket . . . As the story goes, it was a rude event. Not something they'd print in "Brides' Monthly". Brides, on a global level, would have been appalled at the goings-on. With this type of pre-game programming, it's no wonder most marriages are over before the half-time festivities begin.

E.G.B.: I understand you were over thirty before you started to write. And, like Hemingway, you . . .

Chicken: Listen. I'm a Chicken, damn it! I live in a barn somewhere. Down some back road with no main highway around for miles! Every morning it's "Er! Er! Er! Er! Er!". Everybody gets up, walks around, pecks at the ground. Why? I'm not sure. Minerals, perhaps. Our necks move up-and-down-and-back-and-forth . . . _all day long_! Again, I'm not sure why. Some say that it has something to do with making our legs move. I'm not completely sold on the theory, as yet.

E.G.B.: A short time ago, you said "Er! Er! Er! Er! Er!". What exactly does that mean?

Chicken: Well, it means a lot of things. But here's the Webster's definition:

ER! ER! ER! ER! ER! 1) An awakening or warning that the day is about to begin. (English translation – literal) Hey! _HEY!_ Are you deaf?!? I said, "ER! ER! ER! ER! FLIPPING ER!". What do you think this is, "CHARITY WEEK"? There's no such thing as a free lunch . . . for Chickens! Remember that! D'you wanna be a sandwich or what? I didn't think so. Now GET UP!

E.G.B.: Hmm? That's simple enough . . . Now what about your screenplay, "Poultrygeist"? Isn't shooting to commence next month?

Chicken: Another Chicken, maybe . . . I'm not anybody! I wish "Poultrygeist" was mine. Sounds like a great idea. And I wish I could help you out but I gotta go.

E.G.B.: Wait! You're not _anybody_? Are you sure? Could you double-check? I find this very difficult to believe. I wouldn't be asked to interview you if you weren't _anyone_! If you're _nobody_, your name doesn't appear in my column. It just doesn't!

Chicken: Okay, okay, okay . . . relax! I'm not the chicken you want, but at least something good has come out of all this . . .

E.G.B.: Oh, yeah? What?

Chicken: Well, you're on a full page . . . You're telling it like it is and you're not across from a feminine itching ad. That _has_ to be worth something.

E.G.B.: OUT! OUT! GET OUT! A feminine itching ad I can live with; a smartass chicken I can do without!

THIS STUPID HORSE CAN BE YOURS

Surprisingly larger than actual size.

So much emphasis is placed these days on Legend, Beauty, Irrepressible Spirit and Majesty, that it, well, FRANKLY,™ bothered us.

What about the other end of the spectrum? What about the Truly Unattractive, the Clumsy, the Dense and the Pitiable?

FRANKLY,™ we felt that it was about time some of these legends lived on.

Now, the most gifted equestrian sculptor of our time has captured and created FOOL LICKETY SPLIT, an extremely goofy horse—always at top speed, going nowhere and loving it (so he thinks).

His only friend was a little butterfly named Timmy. Timmy was loyal and always at his side until that fateful day when he got in the way of those big, clumsy feet…but let's not get into that now.

Each sculpture will be individually hand-cast and hand-finished. Each will be crafted entirely in rare black (oops, broke another one!) porcelain bisque (not a soup).

What's more, the unusual markings on the forehead and foot of this pathetic little beast will be hand-painted* in pure white; a striking contrast to the rich black bisque (it does sound like a soup, doesn't it?).

What's even more, this sculpture of distinct quality, a tribute to the poor souls of this world, will be accompanied not on a piano but by a certificate of authenticity—of all things!

Isn't it exciting? An original, limited edition sculpture *plus* a vague certificate (piece of paper) which you'll be able to whip out and present to friends when they ask, "What the hell is that?".

FOOL LICKETY SPLIT is truly a work of art which we're convinced that you and your family will treasure forever.

FRANKLY,™ if you don't get it from us, you don't get it from anybody.

*by illegal aliens working ungodly hours in a damp warehouse, meeting outrageous deadlines strictly enforced by a ruthless slavemaster named Konk.

CORRAL №5
PARFUM POUR LES COWS.

THE SPRING

At the dawn of time, in a place that came to be known as "Mom", a marvelous sparkling spring flowed forth, to the delight of mankind.

All the Derrier in the world comes from a similar source.

And, because Derrier is strictly protected*, it's still as clean and pure and delicious as the day you were born.

THE OFFSPRING

Today, you can buy Derrier from the store in regular or natural chocolate.

Derrier. Plain, honest-to-goodness, goodness.

Derrier. It always has been and always will be the Earth's first soft drink.

*unless, of course, some nut drops a bomb.

HOW TO MILK

I t has often been said (and with good reason)
that one never really, fully knows one's spouse until one attempts to fully divorce them.

By the time the police (Domestic Quarrel Squad) have arrived on the scene, gone are the "Hello, Bunny-kins" days and close behind them, on a slightly later train, that weary traveler, "Love Dove Cooing". Now the mere thought of this blissful behavior from yesteryear is enough to make you want to throw up. It is a feeling which you will have for a very long time. Another relationship ends in divorce. It's over...

YOUR EX...
for Everything!

...TO HELL IT IS! Now comes the large task of dividing up, with a reasonable amount of fairness, what's left after the love has gone. Now you get to see what's really in the basement. Now you get to see "The Wrath of Bob".

It's at this stage of the blame where the word "reasonable" suddenly and without warning ceases to mean what the Concise Oxford people claim it to mean: **Reasonable—1**. having sound judgement; sensible; moderate; not expecting too much; ready to listen to reason. **2**. in accordance with reason; not absurd; within the limits of reason; not greatly less or more than might be expected.

After closely studying these definitions, you become aware that not only do they not remotely sound like "Bob", but it also appears that to be reasonable is to give it all away. (To be stupid.)

In the Concise Oxford Dictionary, Divorce Version (updated and authoritative), they have redefined the word "reasonable" in the context of divorce: **Reasonable—1**. once thought to mean fairness within reason but now, through experience, believed to mean "son-of-a-bitch", as do most other words in this specialty volume.

"Son-of-a-bitch" is almost always preceded by "Yer a lowdown" (or the trash equivalent), and is <u>always</u> followed by your spouse's full name. After inspection of the divorce volume's definition, it's blatantly obvious the meaning borders heavily on name-calling. Make no mistake; they are good neighbors.

One week, "name-calling" borrows a cup of sugar from "son-of-a-bitch". The next week, "s.o.b." borrows the hedge trimmers from "name-calling". Their little cooperative arrangement works well. For them!

Cooperation has no place in messy divorce settlements! It has been sent, I'm sure, a letter from somebody's legal counsel instructing it to kindly cooperate and butt out! To live up to the spirit of its name, cooperation most likely obliged.

Oh, great! First sign of trouble and where is "Cooperation"? Across town on Easy Street, sucking lemonade from a tall glass and reminiscing about the "good" old days with its dear friend and colleague of many years, "I'll Share the Blame".

Dynamic duos? Phooey on them! I'll hire myself the best divorce lawyer in town and whoop his butt myself!

Bravo! Cowsmo agrees. Cowsmo says "Take it to the streets!"

"Oops, it didn't work out" and "Oops, it was nobody's fault" is for cowards! You should be concentrating on: "How do I make him pay?", "How do I get the lion's share?" and "How do I get revenge?" Besides, it will probably lead to the most excitement the relationship has seen since "That Day", when saying "I will" and getting to the hotel room seemed to be the two most important things in your lives.

Draw near now, girls, as Cowsmo talks to a divorce lawyer.

My husband says that...

Hold it! Hold it right there! It's question number one and already you're babbling on about what your husband says! Why should you care what your husband says? That's your problem. You always listen to what your husband says. The past ten years have been spent doing what he wants to do. Like only eating in restaurants where he wants to fill his fat face. Like only holidaying in the places he chooses from the travel brochures...

Let me finish. He says we'll save money by using the same lawyer. His. How wise is this idea?

Let me spell it out for you. T-h-i-s i-d-e-a i-s v-e-r-y s-m-a-r-t i-f y-o-u h-a-v-e t-h-e m-i-n-d o-f a g-n-a-t. Do you have an affinity for, or, say, get an uncontrollable urge to fly at light bulbs? No? Good! Divorce might have been the least of your worries.

I think he'll save money, not we'll. He is concerned about I, not we. I say we take him out fast and we take him out now! Hire yourself a good lawyer...someone like myself, for instance. Take him to the cleaners before he has a chance to slither away with everything.

Hank says his net worth is four bucks. I say he has more. Should I believe him?

Think about it! Your poultry baster is worth three. Ya, and the egg flipper is another two dollars. Ah huh, and the knife that never needs sharpening, even if you saw construction boots in half? That had to cost $4.95. That's almost ten bucks right there and we're not even into the important drawers in the kitchen yet. Your take in that haul is already more than ten bucks. Do you want to keep your kitchen utensil showcase or do we continue to play?

I know it's a tough decision and there is some risk involved here. You might lose the baster, flipper and knife, but if we apply some legal pressure, we may be able to work our way out of the junk drawer beside the fridge, do a bit more damage in the kitchen, then in one foul swoop, penetrate the living room. Lord only knows what interesting tidbits we'll find upstairs! Then, if you promise not to turn the light out on me, we'll make a whirlwind tour of the basement and see what we can abscond with.

Why aren't my clients like you? You're lucky this is a magazine or you could be in a lot of trouble.

I'm saying he's worth at least half-a-mill if he's worth a penny. We take him out hard, we take him out fast, we take him out now. Sell everything, split it down the middle. Then we go after his half.

My sister went to a mediator. Should I go to one instead of a lawyer?

I can see divorce runs in your family. Out of curiosity, where does the bulk of your family graze? In my area, I hope.

Look, if your sister jumped in the lake, would you? Ya! Ya! Ya! Okay, other than if the two of you had actually planned a day at the lake. I didn't think so.

Listen, mediators are nice guys. You want to steer away from nice guys. You married a "nice guy". Now look at you. Just look at what all the niceness has done for you.

Mediators try to get lawyers to agree. Does this seem natural to you? Do you want to be pals or do you want blood? Do you want to shake hoofs when it's all over? Can you for one moment picture yourself saying, "Frank, I really must thank you for screwing up the last ten years of my life; it's really been a slice. Maybe we can get together and 'do cud' sometime."

I think we should be concentrating most on getting to his cash. As they say, "Hard and fast from behind."

Friendship does not buy groceries! Try saying, "Hi! Hello! Good day! You're looking chipper!" down at the supermarket and see how many pork chops it buys you.

Ted moved out last Tuesday. What should I do about our joint bank accounts and safety deposit box?

What "joint accounts"? What "joint safety deposit box"? The only "what" I see as being a problem is "what" are you doing wasting time writing to a divorce lawyer who is answering questions in some magazine when you should be in the car racing madly to the bank to remove all the cash and transfer it to "your" account! Likewise with everything that's in the safety deposit box.

The only thing you should avoid doing is banging into the front end of your husband's car coming the other way at top speed because you can bet he's thinking of doing the same thing if he hasn't already done it. In the divorce game, it's often a matter of survival of the quickest.

In the likely event that you get stopped and fined by the police as a result of your maniacal driving, use the ticket as a bargaining tool. After all, Ted is entitled to half. We wouldn't want him to miss out on anything now, would we?

Also, this display of willingness to share will help you get on the good side of the judge. About the only thing in a divorce case that doesn't get split down the middle is the irrepressible feelings of stupidity and anger which follows the non-aggressive spouse for the rest of her life when one party walks away with it all.

Even before Devon moved out, I had an affair. Does that mean I'll get nothing when it goes to court?

What it means to me is that you lean towards being a slut. What are you doing after this article? Would you like to get together for a little drinky or something?

I'm sorry. I'm way out of line. Honestly, I don't make a practice of this. Or rather of divorce I do but I don't make it a habit of coming on to clients. Not that I'm admitting to anything. Nor would I encourage you to admit to anything. That's it! That's the point I was trying to make! I knew there was a point to all of this. I was using myself as an example. Of course, an example. Why didn't I think of that?

Back to the real business of divorce.

Firstly, I can't believe you married a "Devon". Cheating on a "Devon" doesn't count, so don't feel guilty. I would have cheated on a Devon. Devon — sounds thick and creamy to me. Imported, perhaps. I would tend to put Devon on top of strawberries. I can't imagine a woman wanting to sleep with one.

Secondly, if our little friend Devon was shattered as a result of the affair (and I'm sure that he was), the court may treat you more harshly. However, you may be able to get the support of the court by likening your sex life with Devon to sleeping with a bowl of strawberries.

The court, no doubt, will not be able to relate to this and that might work in your favor. Catch them off-guard. Get them rolling around in the hay with a couple dozen big, speckled reds and we get to sit there and watch them wince. On the other hand, if they can relate to that, then they'll know exactly what we mean.

If this doesn't work, we should be able to play up the fact that he never paid any attention to you sexually and after eighteen frustrating months you were forced to have an affair with your divorce lawyer...or someone like that.

Mental cruelty. You may even be able to later sue him for even more money if you are prepared to see a shrink for a while. Now on that note, how about that little drinky? I promise I won't tell Devon. (Tsk! Tsk! Tsk!)

6. Steve says the kids and I can continue to live in the barn. He'll move out but keep paying the mortgage. What if he reneges?

Reneges, eh? So Steve wants to play cards? Well, we'll just see about that, won't we?

You'll want to get a new deck out for this one. The game is called "Abandon the Mortgage". Two or more adults can play. Virtually anything goes. There are five suits: Spades, Hearts, Diamonds, Clubs and Kids. Kids are always trump. Steve thinks he's got the first trick but he doesn't. You not only have the first and subsequent tricks, but you also have the last laugh. The court will frown on Steve.

I would take advantage of the shadow which all of those frowns will cast over Steve and sue him for as much money, property and as many et ceteras as you wish to add to the list. Mental anguish is a nice little tool in court.

Get the cash! Get the kids! Get the picture?

7. I'm an actress. Before I married Chase and when I was, quote, "breaking into the business", I made this little...well, porno movie. Might this little goof-up affect my getting custody of the kids?

Oh, no! The court loves porn stars. And, after all, we all have our little skeletons in the closet. We might be able to enter a plea of, "I'm an actress; it was a role, Your Honor, that's all. As routine as flipping a flapjack is to a short-order cook. I know that *Mr. Wang Meets the Cake Lady* sounds rude, Your Worship, but it was just a name. A funny-sounding name that doesn't mean anything to anybody, anymore."

If the court doesn't buy that plea, we could try a "I was just trying to break into the business". We may be able to get somewhere with this one if we can convince them that sleaze-bag promoters took advantage of you in your moment of desperation.

Wait a second! Did you say porno movie? Maybe you and I should talk about this one in my office. These porno movies can get a bit sticky, if you get my drift. I think I would really rather see either the movie or the script. Now if you could bring either one of these, or better yet, both, into my office, we could go through them together to see if there are any or even some very naughty bits (indeed) in them which might affect the court.

This could get very tricky (perspire, perspire). A later-on-in-the-day appointment might be better, say, 11:00 P.M., when you aren't apt to feel shy and everyone can be themselves and maybe you could wear a red dress or something...

8. Todd says that I can have everything in the garage. Is this fair?

Is there by any chance a Lamborghini and a Maserati in the garage? If not, I hope it is a very large garage. Large enough to pack everything the two of you own in—including the cottage. Unless, of course, you're really into gardening, woodworking and camping equipment. I'm sure the rototiller alone is worth eleven hundred dollars.

Because Todd sounds like a dirtbag, I think it's only fair that he should end up with the rototiller. Counteroffer everything that's in the garage. If he isn't willing to ac-

cept what you offer him, then we'll have to resort to nasty tactics. Financially crippling, nasty tactics.

In the meantime, you could start by phoning the cleaners. Tell them you're bringing in some of your husband's suits. Just make sure Toddy is in one of them.

See you in court.

9. My husband says that because I got the kids and the barn after the aftermath of question six, he wants the family dog, Bark Bark. Is this fair? (And, oh, by the way, he didn't like the little card game you cooked up, either.)

There is nothing worse than a dog hoarder! I hate hearing, "No, it's my dog. Don't touch!". I hear these dog hoarding cases all the time. Believe me, all these guys are sickos.

Let me inform Steve and anyone else out there who's in a similar situation that cash, property or pets—it's all the same in my eyes. Relax! He hasn't got a hope in Hell of getting <u>all</u> of Bark Bark. As long as you bought the dog before you split up. I am assuming that you did. Then you are entitled to half the dog. It's as simple as that. You both, however, may have to settle for a little less barking if it's going to work out for everyone.

Also, it sounds as though Steve still has some wind left in his sails. I'd say he's ready for Round Two. Let's see if we can get some more cash out of him.

See you in court, Steve...Dog hoarder! Dog hoarder!

10. Ned and I separated three weeks ago. He wants the toaster. I'll be danged if I'm going to let him have it. It's a two-slicer. Do we have to split down the middle, even-steven? We're both breakfasty types. What's fair?

Toaster, huh? I can see that this one is going to get dirty if we're not careful. Normally, I'd say take 'em out fast, take 'em out hard. But there might be a way of settling this so you get what you want and Ned gets something he can't use.

Tell him you'd be willing to split the toaster with him. Just be sure that you get to do the cutting. The side you want is the side that has "for one slice only" imprinted on it. That's the side that always works. Ned will be burning his toast either over the element or in the oven, whichever he finds works best for him. Being the "Breakfasty Type", this will bother him. 'Round 7:30 every morning, Ned will be thinking of you.

11. Yes, my wife got the barn and the kids and all I got was the end of the dog you have to clean up after. And I was wondering, Mister Pinhead, in all your wisdom, if you have any idea what morons like you do to others' lives?

Steve, you old dog-hoarder! How about a nice, friendly little game of cards? You're probably wondering right now why a dog who eats nothing, to your knowledge, has to go jobby so many times in one day that it's not even real any more.

12. Why don't you drop by my place some day and I'll show you how we barn train a dog. Bring your nose...we'll need it!

TAXI PADS

FROM HAYFREE

RELAX AND
LEAVE THE
DRIVING
TO US

Some days "traffic" is heavier than others. It's at times like these that you need the kind of heavy duty protection which will allow you to arrive refreshed, on time and without an accident. That's why we've developed Taxi Pads.

Taxi Pads will steer you in, around and through those "heavy traffic" days; safely and at a reasonable fare.

Even if you've never had an accident before, you can probably remember a few close calls. That's reason enough to leave the risk* at home and the driving to us. Because when the meter's running, rest assured; we're in control.

If by chance you do have an accident, we're to blame. This means your insurance rates won't go up; at least not yet.

So next time you're in your local drug store, "hail" yourself a box of Taxi Pads.

Now with the handy little disposable cab. For when more than the meter is running.

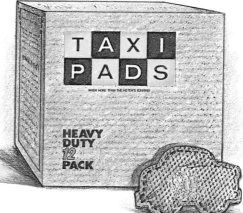

© Hayfree 1987

* Virtually accident-free.

16

How To Tell For Sure

"Do I have a job?"

Many cows are asking themselves this question these days. Many cows get stumped.

You'd better find out soon, kid! You might be working and not getting paid. Or getting paid and not working. You may even be showing up at the wrong job.

Last year, over five thousand cows in the United States alone were fired from the wrong job! Others were fired in groups. This number is astounding. They were shocked. They went into the office only to hear the boss say, "Look, I'm not sure who you are but you're fired. Now get out!"

That was that! Out on their ears, still without work mind you, but oh! the humiliation. Who needs it?

Read on. If you answer yes, no, maybe or even shrug to the following questions, this could mean that you have a job. Wouldn't that be exciting? At the very least, this questionnaire will allow you to organize your day better.

Work force? Or work farce? Which is it going to be?

1. Do you find yourself going out at 8:30 in the morning and then, for some strange reason, coming back home at night?

(a) Yes **(b)** No **(c)** Maybe

2. Have you ever said, "I'm going in there first thing tomorrow morning, clean out my desk and tell them to stick their _____ where there ain't no light!" If you have, has it ever occurred to you why you said this? Have you ever wondered what word might go in the blank?

(a) Yes **(b)** No
(c) Hmmm . . . There _is_ a blank there. I wonder what word goes in it.

3. Does some company give you money every week, two weeks or every month?

(a) Yes **(b)** No **(c)** I can't remember

4. If you answered **(c)** to the last question, what's the matter with you that you can't remember money? Born with a silver shovel in your mouth?

5. Do you, by any chance, go to a big building every day?

(a) Yeah! (she said, rather puzzled) . . . and every day, too.

6. I know this sounds forward and I wouldn't blame you a bit if you didn't want to answer it . . . but . . . do you have a boss?

(a) Yes **(b)** No **(c)** Don't know

7. If you answered yes to Question 6, has this boss ever mentioned that sexual favors have a lot to do with _____ security?

(a) Yes **(b)** No
(c) Have you notified the proper authorities?
(d) Do you know what goes in the blank yet?

8. Does the term "backstabbing coworkers" mean anything to you?

(a) Yes **(b)** No
(c) Just a second. Pull the dagger out of my back first.

9. During the day, other than when you are at home, have you ever tried to solicit products which seem vaguely familiar to you? Answer the phone "Good morning! Cohen-Cohen-Silverstein and Katz"? Discovered advertising brochures in your possession? If you have, can you explain any of this?

(a) Yes **(b)** No **(c)** Daaaaa!

10. Do you constantly hear any or all of the following being said around you: "What's the bottom line?", "I hear you, Ned, and I can sympathize with your situation, but the numbers just aren't there.", "Sorry to let you down, Chief.", "How are you doing, 'Guy'?", "Touch base with me Tuesday and I'll fire the thing off to you straightaway.", "Right, Larry, it'll be on your desk first thing Friday morning.", "Business is so bad that even the ones who never intended to pay aren't buying. Ha! Ho! Good one, Jack."

(a) Yes I do. I just can't remember from where.

11. Do you ever put nail polish on your hoofs in between answering the telephone and talking to your girlfriends? Have you ever taken a look around to see where you are when you're engaged in this activity?

(a) Yes **(b)** No

12. Have you ever read a romantic novel all day long when a Mr. Dempsey was out of an office?

(a) Yes **(b)** No

13. Has someone, by way of an intercom, ever asked you to toddle off to get a coffee for Mr. Heinz Rumble from West Germany?

(a) Yes **(b)** No

14. Have you ever said, "My immediate boss is a total idiot! He's a flake, he's intimidated by me and now I'm on a roll. The President and the whole company stinks!"?

(a) You're damn right I have! . . . I'm just not sure why.

BECAUSE YOU DON'T THE FIBER FIRST

100% NATURAL!

For centuries, blackbirds have enjoyed the secrets of 100% Natural Fiber. Now you, too, can discover the same Natural goodness in a cereal which perhaps you missed the first time through.

From the very first bite of Meadow Treasure Fiber Treats cereal, you'll know why millions have already said, "It has the taste others leave behind."

And because Meadow Treasure doesn't have any sugar, additives or preservatives (the way nature planned it), it's easy on your system all the way down the line.

ALWAYS GET ALL OF TIME 'ROUND...

That's right, one taste of Meadow Treasure Fiber Treats cereal and you'll be heralding the news yourself.

Now enjoy what you missed in convenient <u>new</u> tablet form.

Introducing Meadow Treasure Fiber Treats Tablets—for when you can't take the time to lay down and chew. The same goodness but designed for the cow on the go.

Ask for Meadow Treasure by name; in cereal or new tablets at your pharmacist, grocer or chemist. Just tell him a little bird told you.

MEADOW TREASURE—picking up where nature left off.

COW OLD
DO YOU
THINK
I AM?

Keep them guessing with Oil of Old Hay.®

KOWLÚA
Calfé Olé

Pssst! Hey Gringos! If you don't wanna buy a donkey, maybe Tijuana try a Calfé Olé? It's made with sweet milk, freshly ground coffee and 1¼ ounces of Kowlúa—your favorite coffee liqueur that's imported from funny Mexico.

What's your Lovemaking I.Q.?

DO YOU HAVE ANY EROTIC KNOWLEDGE, OR IS THAT ONLY RESERVED FOR B·A·D G·I·R·L·S ??

The following questions are those most frequently asked of marriage counselors and sex therapists. Each deals with an issue that has created confusion in the love relationships of many young couples.

Remember, answer truthfully or you'll be on a jet plane to "Hell" quicker than you can say "What's your lovemaking I.Q.?"

1. Who gets the most pleasure from our lovemaking?
a. Males
b. Females
c. Our neighbors in the immediate area
d. The hired man (and I wish he'd mind his own business).

2. Does dinner automatically mean sex afterwards?
a. No
b. Yes, but not automatically. We have the manual model.
c. Yes, where I come from it's pretty automatic. Plus I get to write the meal off as a business expense and sometimes the whole evening, depending on the company I'm keeping.

3. Is an erection something they're doing to the big building next door?
a. Yes
b. No
c. I'm a secretary; I don't have time to look out the window!

4. How much time does the average couple? (I know it doesn't sound like a complete question, but give it a try.)
a. Yes
b. No
c. Five minutes
d. The average couple doesn't but I know one that does.

5. Your lover likes you to touch his breasts. Does this mean that he has homosexual tendencies?
a. Yes
b. No
c. No, it probably just means he likes you to touch his breasts. When he wants Ned Smith from next door to caress his breasts, <u>then</u> start asking questions!

6. An erection is a sure sign that your lover is highly aroused.
a. True
b. False
c. Nothing is for sure.
d. It means he has to go to the bathroom.

7. For the most part, male and female orgasms are identical.
a. Completely true
b. Completely false
c. True, in that you are probably both saying identical silly things to each other at that critical and special moment which you would most likely NOT say around Ned Smith from next door when he comes over to borrow the lawn mower. Come to think of it, why does Ned Smith come over to borrow the lawn mower every time we're making love? (Note: I hope Ned Smith's lawn grows really fast or you could very well be in the twilight of a mediocre lovemaking career.)

8. One night, you're thrilled beyond words when your lover caresses you in a certain way. But the next time you make love, the same touch is a total turn-off. What's wrong?
a. You have any one of a number of serious problems.
b. Suddenly he's a GOOF!
c. Nothing is wrong, damn it! How many times do I have to tell you that?
d. The first time he did it, he did it with somebody else. She was thrilled beyond

words! I've never liked it when he says "Gubba Gubba" and then quickly touches my neck. It's a total turn-off! I just don't know what's wrong.

e. Didn't you read (**c**)? I said nothing is wrong, damn it! I don't like using "damn it" any more than you like hearing it but I'll say it again if I think it'll help. Somebody has to shock you back to reality. You've been reading too many of these magazines and you're turning into a neurotic ninny!

9. How often do most couples make lunch? (I thought this quiz was getting just a little too sexy.)
a. Once a day, every day, America should break for lunch.
b. Make lunch, not war!
c. Lunch is a five letter word.
d. Love is never having to say you're lunched. Besides, he already knows that.

10. Who initiates lovemaking most often?
a. You
b. Your lover
c. Ned Smith from next door! Seems like when he's not banging on our front door wanting to borrow something, he's over there going at it! It drives my husband nuts!

11. Overall, how satisfied are most married couples with their sexual relationship?
a. Highly satisfied
b. Moderately satisfied
c. Dissatisfied
d. Give me five bucks and you can take him away!

12. An erogenous zone is:
a. a very scary book by Stephen King.
b. as described by the Highway Traffic Act, "An area where you can't exactly park your car but at the same time, you can't exactly not park your car, without getting a ticket."
c. an area which gives rise to excitement.

13. The "G-spot" is:
a. a short form for "Great-spot". Often when couples go out for dinner, you'll hear someone say, "Let's go to a G-spot this time. I don't care if it's expensive."
b. It's a spot on your body which, when touched, you say one or all of the following: "Gee, that feels good", "Gee, traffic is heavy tonight", "Gee, that feels really good", "Gee, it looks like the police are pulling us over", "Gee, this is going to be really embarrassing", "Gee, why didn't we wait until we got home?"
c. a spot on your body which, when touched, turns you into a Demon Love Goddess in two seconds flat...and I mean it, Bubba!!

d. The "G-spot" is short for Guernseyberg Spot, named after Ernst Guernseyberg, the German gynecologist and sex researcher who discovered it. When this spot is stimulated by deep pressure, it produces vaginal orgasm. It also wakes the neighbors. (How did a gynecologist discover a spot like this anyway? Doctors are supposed to observe the crop, not harvest it!)

14. A "one night stand" is:
a. One piece of furniture in your bedroom which has on it a lamp, an alarm clock and a little porcelain dish containing: a barette, six pennies, a rubber band, two safety pins, a paper clip and a postage stamp.
b. A scumbag! A dirty rat! How could he? Who does he think he is? If I ever see him in public with her, I'll kill him! Maybe I'll kill him anyway! He makes my skin crawl and I probably don't look like Marilyn Monroe, either.

15. You can't get pregnant the first time because:
a. Just because. It's one of life's "big mysteries". There is no possible way the first time and it's <u>so</u> comforting to know.
b. You are allowed one free "first time". It's one of life's "big deals". That's right, one time completely free from the worry of pregnancy. No payments until April of next year and no money down. But hurry, you've only got until October 31st to take advantage of this once-in-a-lifetime offer. Remember, you can't take it with you...Wait a minute! I'm sorry, that's wrong. You can...but why would you want to?
c. Ned Smith told me.
d. It would be horribly unladylike.
e. My mother told me if I ever got pregnant, she'd kill me! So I just can't get pregnant the first time.
f. To everything there is a season. I'll just make sure that I do it in the off-season. That way we won't be bothered by tourists and I'll save money on the air fare, too.

What's Your Lovemaking I.Q.? (Answers)

1. (**c**) The neighbors in the immediate area. You should really try to tone it down. Also, the hired man likes it, too.

2. (**a**) Indeed, automatically. But then, it's the 80's.

3. (**a**) Yes is correct. That's precisely what they're doing to the big building next door.

4. (**c**) Is the correct answer. The average

couple doesn't, but I know somebody who does! Note: For those who guessed five minutes, that was a very good guess, too.

5. (**c**) It probably does just mean that he likes you to touch his breasts. However, I would keep a close eye on Ned Smith. Next thing you know, he'll be wanting to borrow things, which can lead to homosexuality, depending on what it is that he borrows. Just don't let him borrow your husband's tools (one in particular) and you should be all right.

6. (**c**) & (**d**) Boy! Nothing is for sure, that's for sure. And there's a 50/50 chance that in the morning he has to go to the bathroom. So don't think that it's anything you're doing or any perfume you might be wearing.

7. (**c**) True in that you are probably saying identical silly things...And what did I tell you about Ned Smith? Just remember, no tools.

8. In most cases, the answer is (**c**). But in your particular case (at least this time), it's (**b**). Suddenly he's a GOOF! I hate to say it, but I could have told you this a long time ago.

9. (**d**) is the correct answer. Love <u>is</u> never having to say you're lunched. And, <u>yes</u>, he does already know that you are.

10. (**c**) Ned Smith. And he does appear to be hetero, so perhaps there's nothing to worry about.

11. (**d**) is correct. Give me five bucks and you can take him away.

12. An area which gives rise to excitement, especially when you trudge all the way back to your car and discover a ticket on it. Though some will disagree, the answer is, in fact, (**b**), as described by the Highway Traffic Act. (Dumb as it may sound!)

13. (**d**) the Guernseyberg Spot is correct. As far as the neighbors go, tell them to shut up. And if you have any literature on how gynecologists discover spots like this without actually getting involved (aroused is more accurate), I would appreciate it if you would send it along.

14. (**b**) is correct and you <u>don't</u> look like Marilyn Monroe!

15. (**c**) Ned Smith may have told you so, but Ned Smith tells that to everyone. The number of young heifers entering and exiting from Ned's place is perfectly scandalous!

Cowsmo's Wine Suggestions

*Life should be one joyous or miserable moment
immediately followed by another moment of equal joy or misery*

— Chateau du Moment —

Somewhere in the south of France is a tiny winery called *Chateau du Moment*, whose philosophies about cows, occasions and drinking could change the way the world enjoys its wines and each other. COWSMOPOLITAN visited this winery and this is what we discovered.

Chateau du Moment (Castle of the Moment) has developed two lines of wines which are right for the times. *Bovino pour Romantiques* (wine for romantics) and *Bovino pour Psychotiques* (wines for the crazies).

It has taken years of research. Years of selecting grapes for their varying degrees of romantic and psychotic qualities to perfect wines that were made for each other; for the times that were made for each other.

Master wine taster and founder of *Chateau du Moment* says: *"Zee pairsonality of zee wine should match zee moods or desired moods of zee participants and zee mood of zee evening, moment by moment. Zee evening should be a beautiful progression. Whether romantic or psychotic, beauty is evairything. Beauty is in zee eye of zee beholdair."*

"During zee grape selection process, if zee grape deed not make me feel like making love or, on zee othair side of zee coin, if zee grape deed not make me want to hurl appliances at someone, I simply threw zee sucker out. After years of throwing zee suckers out, you eventually have zee grapes zat you want. You also have zee huge mountain of grapes zat you don't want eezer but it's zee price you pay for resairch."

"We sell our wines in zee case of four. Zay must be drank in zee ordair in which zay were meant to be drank. Zis way, zee wine is in control of zee evening — not zee cows! Cows, far too often, jump ahead of zemselves getting things happening before zee time is right. Fanning zee fires zat should not be fanned. Wiz our lines of wines, zee fires fan zemselves when zee time is right. Zee cows concentrate on each uzzer. Whether zee participants are zair for a good time or a bad time is entirely up to them. And zat is zee way hit should be."

Ahh! Cowsmo says, *"C'est magnifique, Chateau du Moment, C'est magnifique! Et bonne chance avec votre product line."*

"Don't drink zee wine before zee time."

Chateau du Here's To Us — $12.95

It's a very dry naive wine. Full-bodied, ready to be plucked. Delicate (I said ready to be plucked). No doubt this wine will not improve with age. Neither will the price be any cheaper. It has been in the bottle long enough. Better start working on it now. (Where the heck is the waiter when you want him?) The bouquet! The bouquet! I forgot the bouquet! Assertive but not aggressive as yet. Seems nice enough looking. It probably doesn't like flowers, so forget the bouquet. Somewhat restrained but the multilayered structure provokes rapturous contemplation.

Chateau du You Want To? — $14.95

A very nice-looking wine. Getting better-looking by the minute. Makes one wonder where this wine has been all your life (Although there is no point in getting carried away. Drinking it once or twice a week is a better idea.). Good heavens, it's a great-looking wine! Only a fool would say no to this one. Most definitely doesn't improve with age and it's not getting any younger in the bottle. Sparkling personality. Becomes more assertive and aggressive sip after sip. Multilayered structure still provoking rapturous contemplation. Where did you park the car?

Chateau du Fumbling For Your Keys — $17.95

The answer is yes, yes, a thousand times yes to this wine (Now where *are* your keys?). The flavor of this prime-for-toppling wine fades quickly so you might want to ask the waiter for a take-out bag and get this bottle home before it fades completely. Unquestionably most pleasant while in the vigor of youth and should not be kept for many years (Who's talkin' years? All I'm asking for is a couple of sips.). Becomes aggressively foxy. Looks more fabulous than I've ever tasted. Must be drunk now or it will become senile (The keys! The keys! I found my keys!).

Chateau du Flailing Around In The Dark — $24.95

Multilayered structure more flabby than originally thought but who cares! Sips better than you ever dreamed possible. Out of the cellar and into your life. Earthy, even a little rough. Perfumed (I think Cowvin Klein.). Great density. Let it breathe sufficiently. If room temperature is too hot, open a window. This superb red wine becomes robust all of a sudden, as if triggered by something. This truly wonderful wine proves once and for all that quality can still be affordable. It has an elegant but "lingering" finish. A tall glass of water might be in line.

The Best of Wines for the Worst of Times

**Chateau du
Glug Glug Glug**   **$1.99**

Very restrained. Very, very restrained. Extremely cheap. Tastes cheap. Feels cheap. Feels cheated. These grapes have been stepped on time and time again by uncaring feet. It started when the grapes were young. The flavor will get aggressive. It, too, is flabby and if it wasn't a wine, you'd swear it was wearing a yellowing tank top. This wine conjures up the words, "shift work". It has a "Don't start in on me!" feel to it. A "Put the kids to bed or I'll wallop them!" look to it. With just a hint of "And I've had just about all I can take of you, too!". That's not to say it won't be interesting. Develops character out of the bottle.

**Chateau du
Shut Up!**   **$2.99**

Oh! Oh! The animal is awake. It has a flavor all its own and more than a slight hint of aggressiveness. Its burly, robust flavor tastes like more. It has a peculiar personality. An unquenchable curiosity (As in "Where were you all day? . . . And don't say shopping!"). If it wasn't a wine you'd swear it just yelled "SHUT UP!" at the top of its lungs. A full-bodied "SHUT UP!" that was directed at you. So what is the attraction of this potentially abusive wine? The yellowing tank top? The seductive, argumentative nature of the grapes? The price? Don't just sit there guzzling — I'm talking to you.

**Chateau du
Toaster Oven In The
Side Of The Head**   **$10.99**

The beast is unleashed. An incredibly bitter wine. Often lingers for days. Even weeks. It has a cloudy sediment which becomes all too clear at once. A delicate taste that has a simple complexity and then . . . your mouth weighs a ton. This is not a young wine. It's a brut. Give this wine a chance to breathe. It has the amazing ability to make appliances sprout wings. And a hint of jealousy which makes you stay with it (yellowing tank top and all). It has a peppery finish.

**Chateau du
I'm Calling The Cops!** **$12.99**

This delightful wine has a sobering effect. Very apologetic in nature. Very "we-can-work-it-out-on-our-own, Officer"ish. Very "the-toaster-oven-just-flew-across-the-room-all-by-itself-as-though-it-were-possessed-by-demons"ish. Very "here,-why-don't-I-put-it-back-on-the-counter-where-it-belongs-and- everyone-can-get-on-with-their- lives"ish. A very believable wine with a dramatic finish. This wine should have gone into the theater and specialized in tragedy. This is a wine you will most likely experience often. It's addictive and seductive (yellowing tank top and all).

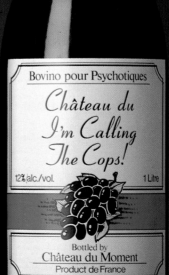

BIG

THE MAXI MAXI FOR THE BIG BIG DAY THAT SEEMS LIKE IT'S NEVER GOING TO END.

SURGEON GENERAL'S WARNING: This MAXI MAXI could be hazardous to your HEALTH HEALTH if used on NON-BIG BIG DAYS* which seem like they're never going to end.

* Okay, Okay, I heard you the first time

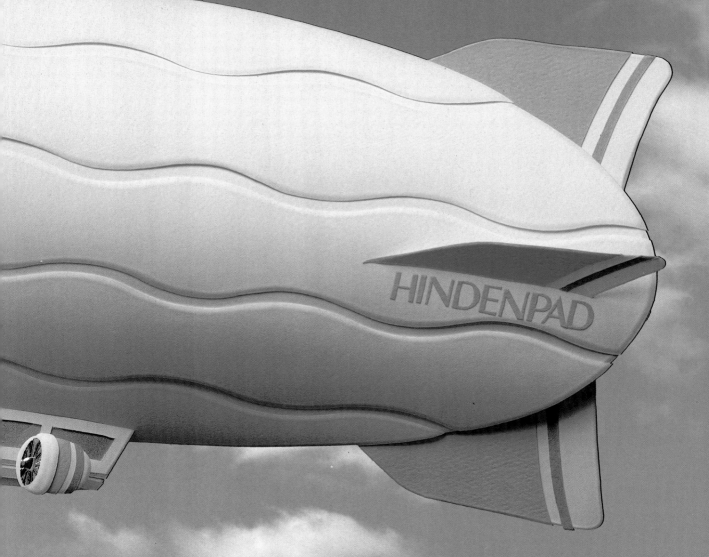

HOOFERS

by

Louis Charolais

The Thistle Toe

The Moo Suede Shoe

The Open Toe C.F.M's

WHO SAYS YOU CAN'T TAKE IT WITH YOU?

The bag for the cow who has everything
and wants to have all of it with her all of the time.

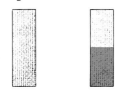
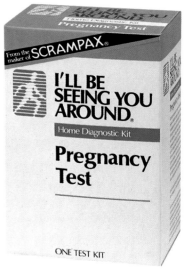
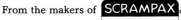

He Loves You Not!

It's 3:08 a.m. You've successfully chewed your hooves off, thrown darts at his photograph and now I suppose it's safe to say that you've been officially stood-up.

All dressed up and nowhere to go. You're not alone. You have a friend in the freezer.

Pizza Time. It's all dressed up with your favorite toppings and in just five short minutes you can be wolfing your woes away.

Yes, "Double Everything" Pizza Time is ready when you are. And that's more than we can say about "What's his name?". And we don't have a mother-in-law that you'll eventually have to take shopping. Now that's a PLUS!

**Pizza Time.
Make it a date
with someone you love**

PIZZA TIME ®
Double Every-Thing!
Ready in 5 minutes

irma kurses
AGONIZING COLUMN

Quiet, please! Irma's got a bone to pick. There might be a little bit of cursing happening here in a second, so I don't want anyone to open their fat trap or blurt out a question until I'm through talking!

First off, the Art Director can suck an egg and soak her head in a water trough. This is the second month in a row (count 'em: one, two) that you put that annoying yellow line right through the middle of my photograph. I'm not sure what your problem is. Are you just being smart or do you really think that a yellow line across my face is flattering?

When I want a yellow line, I'll phone you. I'll say, "Do you happen to have some yellow ink lying around down there in the Art Department? I know it's probably a longshot but I'm curious. I've been toying with the idea of changing my image a little bit and last night I came up with this 'yellow line through the middle of my photograph' idea." Don't hold your breath waiting for my call! Thanks a lot, you idiot.

Next!

I hope you're really happy with yourselves out there in magazine land. For the past God only knows how many years, I've been answering your questions, doing your thinking, living your lives and, in a sense, rolling around in the hay with the stooges you keep moving in with.

Does anyone ever stop and ask Irma how she's doing? No! You're far too busy meeting the wrong guys and getting yourselves up to your necks in hot water! Then you write me "Bleeding Heart" letters. Irrrma, what do I dooooo? My miserrrrable life, Irma. How do I cope, Irrrrma?

I'll tell you how to cope. Use the thing with the horns and the ears on it that's stuck on the end of your neck. Yes, that thing which seems to weigh a ton. Uh huh, it has a mouth and (often), there'll even be a brain. Starts with an H and ends with a D. If you use it regularly, it will really improve your life and cut down on the number of stupid questions which keep flowing into my office and across my desk every day. Do me a favor. No stupid questions! Okay?! Is this too much too ask?

Q. Irrrrrrrma! My husband is having an affair with a giraaaaafe! My dog died last weeeeek. The barn looks like a piiiig sty and I'm getting fatter every day. I haven't worked in yeeeeears! I hate my liiiife and everyone arooooound me. Irrrrma, what should I doooo?

A. There's probably a very good reason why your husband is having an affair with a giraaaaaffe. A giraaaaaffe probably doesn't whiiiine about everything. Stop complaining and start trrrrrrying, you dizzy twit! Didn't you read what I just said about stuuuuupid questions? Ask a stuuuuupid question, you get a stuuuuupid answer!

True, your husband probably likes the way the giraffe neeeecks. And I know you most likely envy the way giraffes reach those faraway leaves on the high branches with such eeeeeease. But I'm sure that if they didn't have those long neeeecks, determined giraffes would learn to climb treeeees. Now get off your butt and kick some. Start with the one you've been sitting on.

Q. Irma. Since you declared war on stupid questions, I've been somewhat hesitant about asking this one. I said to myself, "I'm going to use that big thing that's stuck on the end of my neck to figure out if this is a stupid question. That way Irma won't get all upset and . . ."

A. Lookit! Spare me the thought process involved here. If you have to stop and think about whether or not it's a stupid question, then it's a stupid question. I recognize the signs and believe me, you were going to ask a stupid question. Now would you mind getting off this page?

Q. Irma! I'm at the office! Things have been really crazy here. My boss is a goof and . . . oops! That's the other line ringing. Can I put you on hold for a second? . . . . (beep, beep) . . . . (beep, beep) . . . . (beep, beep) . . . . (beep, beep) . . . . (beep, beep) . . . . (beep, beep) . . . . Sorry about that, Irma! So anyway, as I was saying, my boss is a . . . . . Irma? Irma, are you there? Irrrrr Maaaaa! Don't leave meeeee!

A. Hmmmmmmmmmmmmmmmmmmmmmmmmmmm.

Q. Hi, Irma. Just a quick non-stupid question here for you. I'm a happily married cow with a ten month old calf. Last week (by the time you read this, it will be last year . . . but anyway . . .) I slept with another bull. I am completely disgusted with myself. I've been married for five years and during that time I've never even considered the possibility of having an affair. Then, a friend of mine, who was recently divorced (he finally got rid of that cow!) dropped by my pen to talk about it. He knocked on my pen door, which was really silly of him because you can see over it. So I went over to the door and said, "Who's there?".

He says, "Orange." And I said, "Orange who?". And he said, "Orange you glad I finally got rid of that cow!" We had a good laugh and it really felt great. We played some more knock-knock jokes and then he came in.

My husband was away, of course . . . and Bingo! We began necking like mad almost immediately and then we made ~~lunch~~ love and then he left. After a few hours I felt guilty for what we did. Now I feel terrible. What could possibly have possessed me to do what I did on such short notice? Am I a tramp? I love my husband and I would never want to hurt him. I wish I could say that the sex was bad, but it wasn't. It was horrible!

But Irma, his knock-knock jokes knocked my socks off. We swore we'd never do it again. That was, of course, easy to say at the time. But all I've wanted to do since then is go to the phone, pick it up, dial his number and when he answers, say "Knock-knock, baby!".

If I tell my husband, he'll be devastated. And I'm sure he'll be upset about the sex part, too. Do you think our relationship can be the same as before? Should I breathe a word to my husband? Irma; is there life after "knock-knock"?

A. Well, the "making love" part really isn't a biggy, although you probably should have "made lunch" instead. The "knock-knock" part is going to be a toughy. It would benefit no one for me to try to lead you to believe that it's going to be easy. It will not be. The bull I met before I met my husband was really good at knock-knock jokes. It has taken a long time to forget him. For the first seven years of my marriage, I would go to the phone, pick it up and then slam it down again, sobbing out loud. I'd say, "Damn! Why was he so good at knock-knock jokes anyway?"

He had one really good joke that was similar to the "orange" one that bit you. It started off with "banana" this and "banana" that and then he said "orange". Then I said, "Orange who?". And he said, "Orange you glad I didn't say 'banana'.". Well, I thought the neighbors were going to hear us. I tried to cover my mouth but it didn't do any good. It was simply fabulous. I know what you're going through and I do sympathize.

I think it would be okay to tell your husband about the sex. But I wouldn't leak "knock-knock" if my life depended on it. You can, however, start doing "knock-knock" at home with your husband. Tell him what it does for you. There are lots of good "knock-knock" joke books out there on the market. They range from beginners right up to the professional level. If he practices, he could become very good at it. I honestly think the two of you can make your relationship work. Good luck!

Q. Irma! Irma! Where did you get it? I love it! I just love your new look! I have been considering getting a yellow line right through the middle of my face, too, but nobody seems to have it yet. Are they in the stores or what? Could you give me the address or phone number of the place where you got yours? Thanks in advance. Everything is going great with me. I haven't thought of a stupid question in over a month. I hope you're fine too.

A. Thanks for thinking of me. So you want a yellow line, huh? You can have mine. However, if you insist on having one of your own, write to the Art Director of this magazine. She's probably got a big stack of them down there in the Art Department with my name on them. Tell her I said you could have one. Take a bunch.

COWSMO'S
BACHELOR OF THE MONTH

"Set me free, why don't you, baby."

— MR. AVAIL. A. BULL —

Oh, to be where the cows come across,
To say, "Yo, Bossy", "Whoa, Bossy", "Hello, Bossy".
Pardon my persistance,
thought you'd love my insistence
That I accompany you to the trough.*

*and for that matter, anywhere else you might like to go.

SOMETHING IN THE WAY
HE MOOVES ME

CATTLE
CROSSING

Mr. Avail A. Bull

I'll bring flowers and sweet body lotions.
I'll climb mountains and swim across oceans.
I'm the only one here, dear;
not a chance I'm a steer, dear.
If I were, I'd still go through the motions.

DATA SHEET

NAME: Mr. Avail A. Bull

BREED: Belgian Blue

AGE: 18 months

HUMAN EQUIVALENT: 21 years

BUSINESS: Stock Broker (livestock)

JOB: El Stud-O

INTERESTS: El Stud-O

OTHER INTERESTS: Tennis, football, baseball, but mostly El Stud-O

CAPABILITIES
(FORMERLY EXTRA-COWRICULAR ACTIVITIES) Servicing 50,000 cows per annum (and this ain't no lie).

FAVORITE MOOVIE: Moo Velvet

PET PEEVE: Trying to hold this pen, think and write at the same time ... Maybe somebody could type the rest please.

LOVES (BESIDES EL STUD-O) I love to drive fast, expensive cars when I can get into them without wrecking the upholstery.

The writing of limericks also interests me considerably.

PHONE NUMBER: Out-of-town heifers, call this toil-free line: 1-800-ELS-TUDO

In-town heifers, c'mon over !!

Don't consider this a solid proposal
But I'm more or less at your disposal.
I'm MR. AVAIL A. BULL,
my talents quite saleable,
Plus the door to my pen is quite closeable.

CONFESSION

Cowvin Klein

Questions a Gynecologist Is Most Asked

IT'S OKAY. I'M A DOCTOR

(Not a quiz)

1. "May I leave now?"

2. "Do I have to take my bottoms off, too, Doctor?"

3. "I know that it's going to be good for me, Doctor, but is there another way we can work this ordeal so that it isn't good for you, too?"

4. "Now that I know what your hobbies are, Doctor Rush...What is it that you do for a living?"

5. "Where are the reins on this thing?"

6. "So, Doc," (she said as she slipped her feet into the stirrups), "What time do you reckon we'll be arrivin' in Dodge City?"

7. "Would you mind popping the speculum into the toaster for a few seconds? It's just a little chillier than I'd like it."

8. "You run a hands-on company here, don't you, Doctor Rush?"

9. "Doctor, do you really think 'Pop up on the table and say AHH' is a proper thing for a gynecologist to say to a patient?"

10. "Why are the eyes on that Mona Lisa print moving?"

11. "Are you sure your receptionist's name isn't 'Igor'?"

12. "So then, in all your wisdom and with all your years of gynecological experience, seeing thousands of patients...are you really trying to tell me that *mine* isn't shaped funny? Do you mind if I get a second opinion?"

13. "Call it what you will, Doctor...I prefer to call it a troublemaker. It has brought me nothing but grief! I know this isn't a question *but* it is a fact of life."

COWSMO

ARIES (March 21 – April 20)

Aries, up until the 20th, Mars will allow you to seize the opportunity. He's out of town. Seize the kids, seize the bank account, find the keys and get the heck out of there before he comes back. Come to think of it, where are the keys? I left them . . . no, I didn't. The maid . . . we don't have a maid . . . Why didn't I buy one of those stupid beeping key-finders everyone else in the world did? Because they go off in restaurants when somebody clacks their teeth three times, that's why! Just find the keys! The guy's an animal — he's probably turning the corner at the end of the lane right now.

Aries, someone has been removing money from or not contributing to the office "on-your-honor" snack dispensing unit. If you're stealing, Aries, put it back! If you're not contributing (which is still stealing), cough it up! It doesn't look good on a resumé. We don't need "It's Mr. Snack Time" coming back to haunt us now, do we?

Your lover (not to be mistaken for your husband) is also going through some troubled times. Be spontaneous. Go over and make dinner for him. Candlelight, wine, "dessert". It'll lift his spirits. As far as getting out of the barn . . . tell Ted* (not to be mistaken for your lover) that you have some unfinished business to take care of down at the office. Isn't that always his line? If the shoe fits, wear it. If they look great, buy them!

*Ted, where applicable

TAURUS (April 21 – May 21)

Taurus is a Bullshooter! Hee! Hee! Hee! Hee! Hee! Hee! Just kidding, Taurus. If I have a favorite, you're it.

Can you spell "sex"? I hope so, because that's what you're going to be doing for the next month. It will seem like every bull in the county has finally come to his senses. And ALL at the same time, too. It *will* be overwhelming.

However, you should resist the temptation to dominate a lover on the 28th. It's only for one day; surely you can wait that long. To make the wait a little sweeter, why not declare the 29th to be "National Domination Day". Then really go all out. Cat-and-mouse him until there really isn't much point in continuing. (Or at least until the Police Crowd Control Unit is called in to announce over their megaphones, "All right . . . Everyone clear the area! Come on! . . . Come on! Everyone's seen somebody tie their lover to the back of a pick-up truck before! Come on! . . . Come on! . . . Go back to your stalls!")

Between the 6th and 14th you feel the need to assert yourself. Wait it out. If left alone, assertiveness will eventually go away. On the 12th, Mars stirs up suppressed conflicts with mate. Tell Mars to keep its fat trap shut.

Get rid of that clinging friend! Cling! Cling! Cling! Complain! Complain! Complain!

GEMINI (May 22 – June 21)

Will face financial and sexual blocks with lover. He blocks the finances, you block the sex! Blocking the finances has a strange tendency to go on and on if not kept in check. Sex-blocking should occur simultaneously with blocking of finances. (If you're smart, it *always* does.*) I don't think you need a reminder about who is in control. Be straightforward. No more moo-la, no more "dessert".

Around the end of the month, as you open your apartment door, you come face to face with a total stranger . . . Oh! . . . I'm sorry. No, you don't! I forgot about the full-length mirror in the hallway.

A period of self-questioning could be very helpful now. Just keep the answers short and to the point. One to six words will be fine. Do it when nobody else is around.

On the 28th, though it will have nothing to do with you, Mars helps Mercury girl make demands of her own. Ya, right! And Jupiter helps the cow jump over the moon, too.

* Remember, you owe "strange tendency" nothing.

CANCER (June 22 – July 23)

Crabs exert persuasive charm on job interviewers. Well, that certainly sounds like a first, doesn't it? You don't by any chance have crabs, do you? You do? Then you've got the job. Ah yes, the persuasive power of crabs.

You'll go outside on Wednesday but then you'll come running back just as the phone is ringing. Drat! Wrong number!

A journey could be relaxing *or* a nightmare. Full moon reveals apparent lies flying around the office about you and Mr. Baxter. It's time you and Baxter had lunch together to straighten things out. Only *this* time, have lunch.

If you don't have a therapist, look under "Feldman" in the phone book. Don't look under Goldstein; they're film producers. They'll want your body. Remember: Feldman, mind / Goldstein, body / Feldman, mind / Goldstein, body.

On the 17th, don't use your Visa to pay off your MasterCard. They have a name for that — it's against the law.

True, the boss' wife does chew her cud like an ox. I know that. We all know that! Let's not make a habit of going around reminding everyone, okay?

Lengthy chat with lover becomes more intimate until 9:30. Then he mispronounces "vichyssoise". This cools things down rather abruptly. (What a dingbat!) But then things heat back up considerably at his mention of an around-the-world vacation with unlimited spending (not as big a dingbat as you thought). However, at 9:36, another mispronounciation, this time "genre", and you send him packing his bags. Who were you kidding? He's a dingbat; always has been, always will be.

LEO (July 24 – August 23)

Until the 23rd, the Lioness will be overstocked with suitors. Have a sale. Slash prices — mark everyone down 60% or more. The ones which don't move, dump.

February is a good month to pay the rent. Do it! You'll feel better . . . unless we're talking about July's rent. Then you should forget what I said about February.

August 3rd, you're thrown out of your apartment. The landlord didn't buy the "I'll-pay-you-at-the-end-of-February" routine. Leo doesn't listen . . . Leo takes her lumps. If you have a gummy smile, look into surgery.

Snappish coworkers and brewing rivalries along with a demanding schedule threaten to boil over at the office unless you pay them $300 in small, unmarked bills. Pay them, for God's sake! Chances are they've found out about that little rendezvous with Mr. Baxter. That's the last thing you need surfacing. (Hmm? Baxter sure gets around.)

Your mate's finances could be dwindling — better start looking around for someone a little more stable. Then, when the time is right, it's au revoir Monsieur Dwindle, bonjour Monsieur Cash.

Last month's tension is this month's full-blown raging fight.

VIRGO (August 24 – September 23)

Virgo, your prescription for Valium needs to be renewed; you've only got five left.

Pardon?

I said your Valium prescription needs renewing. Try shaking the bottle, you'll know what I mean.

I know that!! I don't need you telling me . . . Scaring the hell out of me!

You don't have to get huffy, Virgo. I thought I'd mention it, that's all. Also, I hate to be a bug, but if you take a look at the label, you'll notice it says "to be renewed zero (0) more times". I guess this means another trip to Dr. Goldstein. You really should try Feldman. Goldstein is more of a body kinda guy, if you catch my drift. He has those penetrating eyes which stir and awaken other emotions which shouldn't be summoned to the podium — not even in the privacy of a doctor's office. I was telling Pisces the other day . . .

Oh, shut up about Pisces! They're nothing but opportunists. Optimistic go-getters. They can keep their intriguing opinions, their sultry lovemaking, their moxie, their so-called creative pursuits. Yes, Pisceans can take their windfalls along with some whopping bills near the end of the month (Ha! Ha!) and blow them out their noses.

On the 25th, lovemaking is rapturous. But only on the 25th, so don't get too used to it. On the 26th, it's straight back to the regular irregular routine of once every two months. Don't let it get to you. Remember, 65% of the rest of the world is going through the same thing.

LIBRA (September 24 – October 23)

Sultry lovemaking is on the horizon around the . . . no, wait . . . No, I'm sorry. Sultry lovemaking is on the horizon for Pisces child. Guilt and laundry are on your horizon. I'm sorry, but that's the way it is.

I know! I know! It's not as much fun as sultry lovemaking, but . . . All right, I'll make a concession. The best I can do is guilt and band practice. Okay then, guilt and aerobics and that's my final offer!

HORRORSCOPES

Yes, I'm a Pisces. But that has nothing to do with anything. It isn't fixed. That's the way the chips fell. I'm entitled to some sultry lovemaking now and then. If you want to argue, I can change aerobics to backstabbing coworkers JUST LIKE THAT! Okay then, backstabbing coworkers it is.

Steamy stay-at-home encounter turns out to be a towel over the head, face over the medicated vaporizer in an attempt to loosen phlegm from your chest. Two colds in three weeks! Where is the romance? Where is the laughter?

On the 7th, you find intellectual stimulation by reading the T.V. guide: Channel 6 at 11:00 P.M. Movie of the Week: A HEIFER NAMED ALICE. Alice, an aerobics teacher, leaves her small hometown somewhere in the mid-west for New York where she forms a punk rock band called Alice and the Beefsteaks. Chaos ensues. Where is the romance? Where is the laughter? Where is the guy I knew?

SCORPIO (October 24 – November 22)

Scorpio rules the gonads . . . Na! Na! Na! Na! Na! Na! Scorpio rules the gonads . . . Na! Na! Na! Na! Na! Na!

SAGITTARIUS
(November 23 – December 21)

Sagittarius? Psst! Sagittarius? Psst!. . . Sagittariuuuuuus! Hey, Stupiiiid! I'm going to throw a pillooow. Maybe even a damp raaag if you don't wake up. SAGITTARIUS! Don't make me start talking about inadequate birth control, Sagittarius. It's easy as pie for me. Remember, I've got the typewriter. Starting Monday morning, you're going to begin eating like a piiiiig. Where's my dictionary? I wonder how I spell nymphomaniaaac? SAG-I-TTARIUS!! Aha! I thought that last one would get to you! Everyone's secret fear. Try the damp rag threat; nothing. Mention nympho once and it's wakey-wakey Sagittarius. Where was I? Ah, yes.

Sagittarius, around the 15th, globetrotting Archers should storm into your home reeking of cheap wine, yelling, making rude gestures and spewing demands.

"Bring us the young one . . . the heifer. Deliver unto us the one they call Lady Marjorie, Duchess of Uxbridge!"

Do not be distressed. The police *will* drag them away. However, this sort of goings-on is enormously on the increase these days. Imposing? Somewhat. I myself like to think of it as dinner theater.

On the 26th, a well-traveled foreigner will flatter you on the bus. You are amused by his persistence. You are intrigued by his constant hoof motions. He keeps patting the shirt pocket over his heart then touches his lips. He repeats this time and time again. He wants dinner . . . I think . . . No . . . He wants to kiss you . . . No . . . He loves you . . . No . . . He wants a cigarette . . . Yes! Yes! He's out of smokes. Yes, and he needs a light, too. Oh, well, it might have been that unforgettable night — sorry, not this time.

And finally, on the 21st, Sagittarius, for 100 points and the game: Is the proper term for a quantity of geese, (a) a gaggle? or (b) a covy? A gaggle or a covy? . . . Time is running out, Sagittarius . . . (buzzer sounds). I'm sorry, Sagittarius, it is, in fact, a gaggle.

And if you remember last week on the show, Pisces, of all signs, guessed a covy of crows. That was not correct. It is, in fact, a murder of crows. However, despite the setback, Pisces made an amazing comeback to win the game and, of course, will be in our final roundup next month. Enough about Pisces.

But now I'm sad to say that we're going to have to say goodbye to Sagittarius. You did manage to rack up $3600 in cash. That's yours to keep. As well, you won the very lovely Orion's Belt collection; again, yours to keep.

One of the up sides of saying goodbye is that we get to say hello to a new sign and contestant. Please make welcome . . . CAPRICORN (applause).

CAPRICORN
(December 22 – January 20)

Hey, Shabby! Yes, I'm talking to you, goat face. I think it's about time we had a little chat about the cleaning rags you call a wardrobe. Spruce up, kid! No wonder everyone else is getting the attention.

Check to see if your spouse has accidentally left the gas on in the stove. He has? Oops! You'll have to remind him not to be so careless next time. Anyone can make a mistake but, good heavens!, three times in one week? And always when he's out?

A misunderstanding about what was thought to be a joint bank account turns into a two-day marathon of "It's Smine" . . . "It is Snot!" . . . "I said, 'It's Smine'." . . . "It is Snot.".

You may want to end it all by using this really good comeback line. It always seems to work for me in Smine/Snot situations. Try saying: "If it's snot smine, how come it's got smine name on it?" That should shut him up.

Chums with soul-wrenching problems flock to you for sympathy. Don't let them in! Pretend you're the cleaning lady. Speak in broken English through the letter slot. Say something like this: "She gone away now. She nut come beck for two weeks. I dunt know where she go. She shacked up, maybe. I must go feed dog now before he starts to barking (make barking noises). Now see what you do. Dog starts to barking, next he be getting sick on the carpet . . . Tank you. Yes, you have savvy, too. Tank you."

AQUARIUS (January 21 – February 19)

Your mate may be too distracted by job or money problems or . . . or . . . not Miss Fletcher at the office? Of course! It all works out! The weekend at the cottage. The sudden cancellation of birthday dinner. Oh, she's a little hussy, all right. And that little fish is about to swim off with your luscious hunk of Leo. Gemini Cricket, kid!

You're going to have to get crafty and send a curious Aquarius over to inform her to stay away or you'll Sagittarius her hair out with your bare hoofs. End of cosmic encounter!

Between the 16th and the 22nd, yielding to a lover's wishes can strengthen your relationship. On the other hand, yielding to his wildest desires can prove to be humiliating. So what's it going to be? Peace and harmony or humiliation and disgust? You'll figure it out. But will you make the right decision? Time will tell.

On the 23rd, Financial Conflicts sabotage Intimacy. Intimacy retaliates, landing a solid bust in the mouth. Financial Conflicts calls the police. Intimacy gets a free ride downtown in the cruiser to the cop shop. Financial Conflicts presses charges.

I ask, Where the HELL is Justice? I said, Where the HELL is Justice? If Financial Conflicts had kept its big nose out of Intimacy's business, none of this would have happened.

(Enter Justice, rather wound up.) Hold it! I saw everything! I saw it all from right over there! In fact, all of you . . . I want all of you over there in the corner. (Gestures with revolver, his gun hoof shaking.) Don't any of you police try reaching for your guns. We don't want any accidents. Besides, I've already jammed them. So one of you wise guys wanted to know where Justice was? And obviously badly enough to shout HELL all over the page in capital letters. Well, you got me!

Now what are you going to do about me, huh?

You wanna know where I was? (Waves revolver, pointing it at everyone.) Well, Justice has a bit of a drinking problem, okay? Does anyone here care? (Everyone quickly nods.) Sure everyone cares when they're staring down the barrel of a .38 . . . Suddenly everybody's a little 'care package'. Well, I'm tired of it! (Justice to Intimacy) Come on, kid. This place is sick. I'm taking you outta here. (Justice is now down. Justice and Intimacy exit, leaving Financial Conflict and Police staring at each other in astonishment. Curtain falls.)

PISCES (February 20 – March 20)

Well, well, well. The long-awaited bout of sultry lovemaking is finally upon us. I hope you really appreciate it, Pisces, because it's already caused enough trouble in this bloody article. Ride 'em, cowgirl.

Also, your 30-day supply of breast enlargement ointment has run out. The moment of truth has arrived. Are you completely satisfied or do you return the empty tube to the manufacturer, knowing full well this means "they" are never going to be any bigger? Or do you join the "millions of satisfied customers" group whose lives have not changed forever but were too chicken-shit to admit that a scam is a scam is a scam?

Look at it this way. The extra moisture never hurt them a bit. You have your money back. And, most important, you aren't a chicken-shit. Congratulations.

IF YOUR EVERYDAY* MAXI LOOKS LIKE THIS, YOU COULD BE HAVING A FEW TOO MANY ACCIDENTS.

It looks incredible, doesn't it? And you're probably wondering why we put fins on it, right?

Introducing Sometimes®, a whole new zany kind of protection. We know you're asking, "But when do I wear them?". Let's just say... "Sometimes". They're for when always is too much and never is not enough.

The revolutionary Sometimes®. The one with the fins.

"But why do I need fins?" You don't. The fins are a bonus. They don't cost anything extra. They're not for anything in particular. They look nifty, okay? We like 'em — you'll get used to them. Now shut up and let me finish this ad. That's right, new Sometimes® with the patented, marginally-protective dry-weave surface lets you glide through those moderate days with only a slim chance** of an accident.

But why does it look like a hammerhead shark? Because it comes out of the mold that way. GEEZ!!

sometimes

Unscented

12 MAXI PADS

* not recommended for every day. hence the name Sometimes®

** virtually a slim chance of an accident

WE'VE GOT YOUR MIND, NOW GIVE US YOUR BODY

VALIUM

The Air Fare's On Us ... The Rest's On You !!

GOTTA-GET-A-WAY SLEEPSTAKES

Introducing the Valium Frequent Flyers "get-a-way-island-retreat-bonus-point-advantage" program. When you fly Valium's "Friendly Skies", you qualify to take advantage of somebody else for a change. US!

Now, with every purchase of Valium, comes an exciting little easy-to-remove advantage sticker. Look for it under the lid. You can't miss it. It says "This is a bonus point. Store it in a safe place. The junk drawer beside the refrigerator where you keep the knives is perfect. P.S., your husband's a creep. Just five more bonus points and you're outta here!"

It's as simple as that. Just six little bonus points and it's up, up and away. Nothing beats hanging in like getting out. And now, with the bonus-point advantage program, it's never been easier.

Give us your body and we'll give you the return air fare *plus* a mitt full of get-a-way bucks to spend while you're there to help offset the cost of your stay.

Ahh! Life without stress. Face-to-face with reality in the not-so-stressful atmosphere of an island paradise.

Valium. We take you there...and now, we bring you back, too.

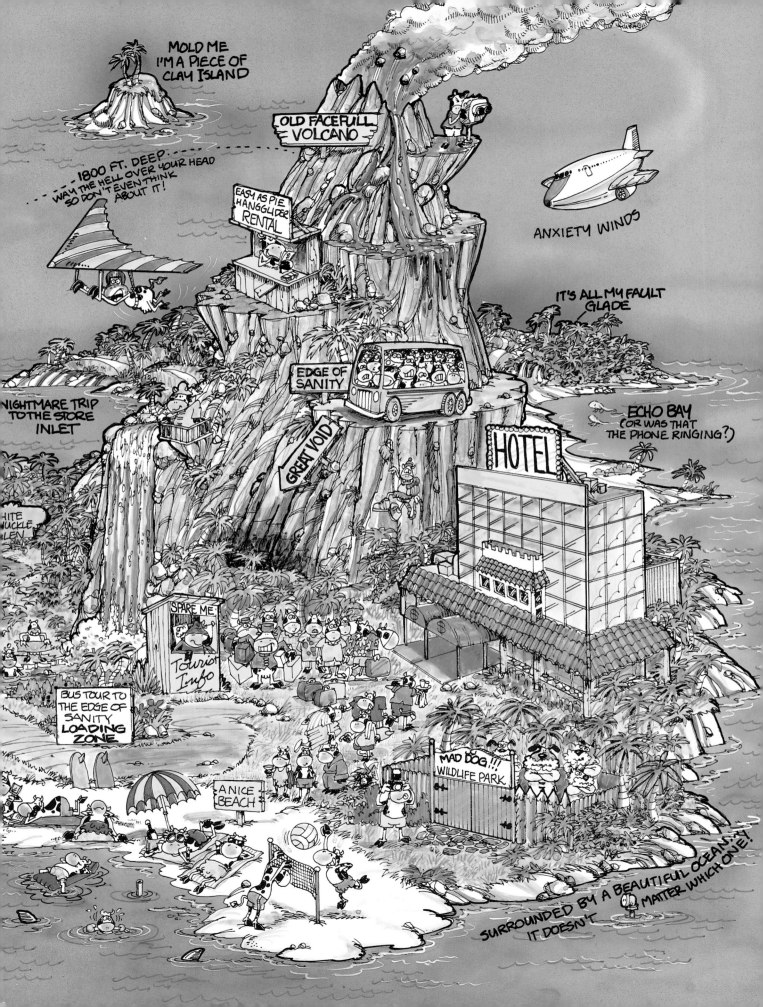

JOIN DE-CLUB

De-Aging Specialists.

When skin begins to show its age, it means you're getting older. It happens to everyone, eventually. It's de-pressing.

New skin layers–formed rapidly when you were younger–now take longer to surface. So the top layers stay on too long. Far too long. (Relax, you've got time to make one last quick trip to the store.)

Dermatologists know one sure way to help reverse the look of aging. But they won't tell us. Believe us; we've begged and we've badgered. They no-telly! No way! No-key Dokey! Uh uh!

However, the next-best-kept secret is no secret at all. Skinique 7 Day Scrub Club Cream.

Millions have already enjoyed its benefits. More convenient than a belt sander, and it doesn't have a plug.

Try it every day for a week. 7 Day Scrub Club wakes up sleeping skin . . . (Okay, everybody up! We don't need no lagging layers lying around here!) It speeds off tired old top layers, encouraging younger skin to renew itself. Leaves you smooth and soft as a baby's . . .

Find it–plus get a free skin analysis with the Skinique Computer–wherever Skinique is sold.

The 7 Day Scrub Club Cream makes skin look younger. It's dependable. It's de-aging. And you can throw away de-sander.

SKINIQUE

Allergy Tested
100% Fragrance Free

At last, something for the big jobs.
Estée Fodder introduces

Patch Kit in a Drum

'cause sometimes you need lots.

What makes skin perfect? To be honest — nothing.
What makes a skin care product perfect for the tough jobs?
In a word — LOTS.

In just twenty short minutes after trowelling on Patch Kit
in a Drum, your appearance will be:

- **measurably thicker**
- **measurably smoother**
- **and visibly restructurized.**

Scientific tests, including sonar, prove it. The fluffy-light formula feels so wonderful you won't remember you have it on until somebody yells out, "Hey, Tammy! How's* Jim doing?"

Patch Kit in a Drum.
IT REALLY WORKS

*Or is that "who's"?

ESTĒE FODDER

MOO YORK • LONDON • PARIS

THE OUTFIT THAT

In the old days, showing up naked for work was not only an accepted practice but was commonplace. Even in the most progressive office of the day, a hat alone would suffice. Times have changed. A hat alone will no longer suffice.

In today's competitive business world, it takes more than wearing a basket of fruit on your head to get noticed. Cows who have not been able to adjust and adapt to the new dress trends in the workplace are finding themselves left out in the cold. No wonder goats and even ducks (which is a complete joke!) with a flair for fashion are snapping up jobs right out from under the noses of these more than qualified cows.

That's right. Your inability to get along with coworkers, your poor grammar, your lack of initiative, lack of supervisory skills and poor timing no longer guarantees you your job.

GOT ME THE JOB!

Stepping on the boss' tail and going "good old number-two" on his forehead (as if you didn't know he was there) when you're all jammed together over in the feedlot will not get you sufficiently noticed to win that all-important promotion.

You can't just leave that promotion up to chance. You have to plan for it! It's called "dressing for success".

The outfit that gets you noticed is the outfit that gets you that job. The ensemble below is a sure-fire way of getting noticed. These are the items which Cowsmo believes employers are looking for this year. You most certainly don't have to go through the expense of blowing your nest egg on all of it. Owning even some of them should not only put you in line for a promotion but also make you the envy of the entire office!

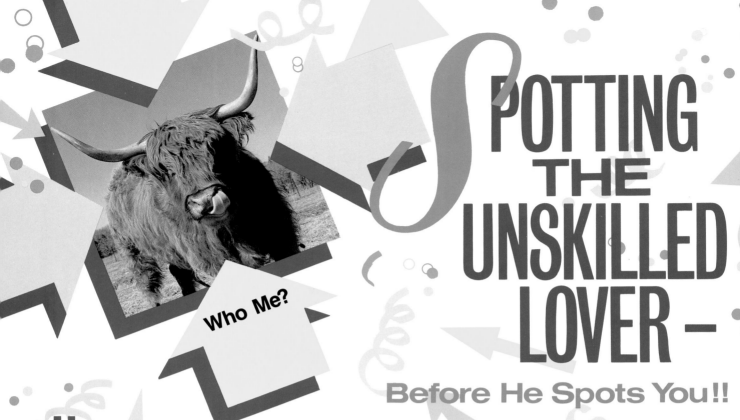

Who Me?

SPOTTING THE UNSKILLED LOVER –

Before He Spots You!!

He's gentle, considerate, devoted . . . but an erotic nincompoop. Is all that gentleness, consideration and devotion worth the "Mr. Lights Are On But Nobody's Home" treatment you get in the bedroom? If so, why don't you and Martin* go away someplace nice and be gentle together? Perhaps a library would be an appropriate spot. You should take out a whole bunch of books because you'll have plenty of time to read in bed. However, if a healthy, active sexual partner appeals to you, learn how to spot the unskilled lover — before he spots you.
*Martin where applicable

Profiles in Unproficiency

Mary and Martin had been living together happily for a year. Don't get me wrong, Martin *is* a nice guy. He has lots of sterling qualities — that sort of thing. But Martin would kiss and caress Mary only on the couch. It was very frustrating for Mary. She'd sit impatiently in the chair on the other side of the room. "Martin," she'd say, "I don't think my couch is getting a lot out of this little session. You can kiss its arms and rub its pillows if you like, but I think you're wasting your time. True, it's probably good, safe practice for when you try tackling something more aggressive, like the food processor out there in the kitchen, but at present, it's . . . it's very frustrating for me to watch. And if you had any sense, it should be extremely embarrassing for you to perform." (The kitchen is the unskilled lover's equivalent to a chain-and-leather bar.)

Sorted Things Out

It's comforting to know that Mary and Martin eventually parted company. Mary moved out, taking only her clothes. Martin couldn't bring himself to part with his furniture. Martin *did* marry her couch.

They seem to be very happy together; the couch *is* pregnant and, according to Mary, expecting "a chair" in February. Martin was hoping for a footstool, but after the tests, the doctor said it was most definitely going to be "a chair."

YAHOO! WE'RE IN THE RODEO NOW! (formerly called "IDENTIFYING AND HANDLING THE SUSPECTS")

The Mr. Fix-It Type

He always has his tools ready (with the exception of one). He believes that everything should be fixed. Except for the cat. It should abstain and maintain. Should you decide to accept this work-order, you will save thousands on tradesmen. You will live in frustration in a squeakproof, leakproof environment.

The Mr. Did I Tell You What Larry Did At Work Today Type

These guys are workaholics. They become married to their work to cover up the emptiness in their personal lives. Any time you want to hear another "Larry" story, just mention the frightening words, "Passionate Lovemaking".

Chapter 531. The day Larry arrived at work two hours late, wearing a lamp shade on his head. All the boss could do was laugh and say to Larry, "Larry, get outta here and go sell some computers, you big loveable nut, you!"

Steer clear of workaholics. All they do is talk about work. You'll either be alone all the time or, if you do manage to change them somewhat, you'll be together all the time. That might be even worse.

The Mr. Keeps His Distance Type

These guys don't want to risk accidentally bumping your udder with their leg. They choose to conduct the evening from a safe distance. A hundred yards or more is quite safe to them. Not exactly an intimate, candlelit dinner for two unless you call opposite ends of a football field intimate. It makes passing food exciting but tedious.

"Martin! Go for the long bomb! Martin! . . . Dinner roll in the end zone!" And so on and so forth.

I would ask to be excused from this dinner table and get while the going is good.

The Mr. Inquisitive About Every Little Knickknack In Your China Cabinet But Not About Your Favorite Little Knickknack Not In Your China Cabinet Type

He finds a piece of paper to be the most fascinating thing in the world when you do something really gross . . . like show affection.

"Where did you get this penny?", "Is that a button on your blouse?" and "What was your grandmother's middle name?" is a random sampling of what you can look forward to.

We suggest you get a little inquisitive yourself and look for someone who is a tad less inquisitive.

The Mr. Don't Talk About Guppies, Yuppies Or Puppies Type

Mention any one of the above three to this guy and he could be in trouble. Even though it was an innocent mistake (and you couldn't possibly have known), Guppies, Yuppies and Puppies remind him of sex. He will become very uncomfortable.

He feels that Yuppies should restrain themselves, discover a hobby or find some other form of recreation. Guppies should do the same. And Puppies are just the result of something rude which took place between two consenting adult dogs (this does not let Puppies off the hook — somebody should have known when to quit).

Run for your life from this guy!

The Mr. Conversational Bumbler Type

One look into your beckoning baby-blues and his mouth automatically fills with popcorn. Mention "puppy" a second time and he clams. He remains silent when he should speak up and rambles nervously when quiet is called for. He avoids eye-contact in public places for fear you will unjustifiably slap him right there in the restaurant *or* get up and do a sexy dance around the dining room and break into the old favorite boyhood schoolyard rhyming song, "Oh, Away Down In France Where The Heifers Wear No Pants".

He's Like A Kitten With A Ball Of Wool

Whether he's the newly-divorced male, the younger bull or the workaholic, something is preventing him from developing on a sexual level. Unless you're prepared to take the time to baby him along, these kittens are better off playing on their own. No amount of catnip is going to change these kitties into tigers overnight.

MOO-PRODUCTS – TOOLS FOR GIVING!®

A COLLECTION OF FIRST CLASS CONTEMPORARY PRODUCTS

THE ORIGINAL WOODCHUCK BOMB®

Form Teams * Compete for Prizes * Fits in Pocket * Toss & Run Convenience *

Get in on the fun that swept Europe and is fast becoming a sport here in America. Woodchuck Bombs®. The latest fun way to kiss-off those pesky little critters who riddle the pasture with those holes we're constantly falling into.

Now you and the whole family can have a "Hole Lotta Fun" while waving goodbye to sprained ankles and maybe you'll even win yourselves some prizes to boot.

Woodchuck Bombs® are so compact they'll fit in your back pocket. Take 'em anywhere! When you come upon a hole, simply light, toss and run. Then, KA-BOOM!!

The contestant who racks up the most points (Woodchucks) wins. Just read what everyone's saying:

Jersey Journal — "Bonjour fun . . . Au revoir Woodchucks. Beaucoup de fun!"
Holstein Journal — "Greatest game since Meadow Ball and more fun, too."
Moo Mar Khadaffy — "How much wood could a Woodchuck chuck if a Woodchuck could . . . KA-BOOM! Great starter kit. 'Hole lotta fun' ".
Johnny Woodchuck — "So it was 2:30 Saturday afternoon. I'm down in my hole watching some television when, KA-FLIPPING-BOOM . . . Our world caves in. I got three good legs left — one's just a stump. Mildred wasn't so lucky. I can say they've been just a 'Hole Lotta Fun!' for us."

Just **$7.99** at finer farm supply stores everywhere.

▼

NO MORE SUCKING UP TO MOM! ▶

Calf-Eteria® makes mealtime a breeze and gives Mom a break. This durable nipple drinker pail gets those little suckers going on their own earlier, gets you back to work earlier and saves you a bundle on day care.

Calf-Eterias® patented "Looks Just Like Mom's"® teat-nipple delivery apparatus gives hours of sucking enjoyment and nourishment to the newly weaned hommy in your life.

Nothing looks like or satisfies quite like Calf-Eteria®.

From **$39.95** at finer feed stores everywhere.

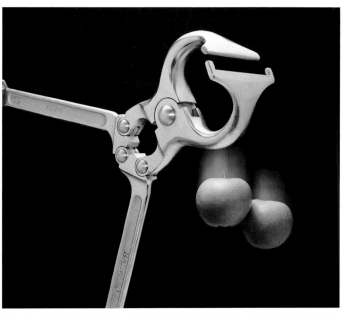

THE LATEST IN FEMININE PROTECTION

Introducing the "Honey, Are You Awake?"® neutralization unit. For when you know he's been slipping around and he doesn't deserve a second chance.

Now you can change his bad socializing habits from fast-forward to neutral in just seconds with the "Honey, Are You Awake?"® neutralization unit. (Yes, folks, that's what I said. It's the "Honey, Are You Awake?"® neutralization unit.)

Makes tossing and turning, rolling over, flicking on the light, checking the alarm clock, going to get a glass of water, slyly looking out the window, checking the alarm clock and saying "I'll kill him!" a thing of the past.

Comes complete with squeezer unit and two practice apples.

Now here's the good part. It's only $129.99. A small price to pay for peace of mind.

Just read what everyone's saying about it:
Holstein Journal — "More fun than Meadow Ball and Woodchuck Bombs® put together."
Moo Mar Khadaffy — "Great starter kit. 'Whole lotta pain.'"
Johnny Woodchuck — "Looks like a 'Hole lotta fun!' for somebody."
Ms. Magazine — "Chuckle! Chuckle! Chortle! Chortle! Ha! Ha!"
Daily Moos — "More than the price is right."
"Honey, are you awake?" . . . "I AM NOW!!!"

EXTERIOR / INTERIOR DESIGN

56

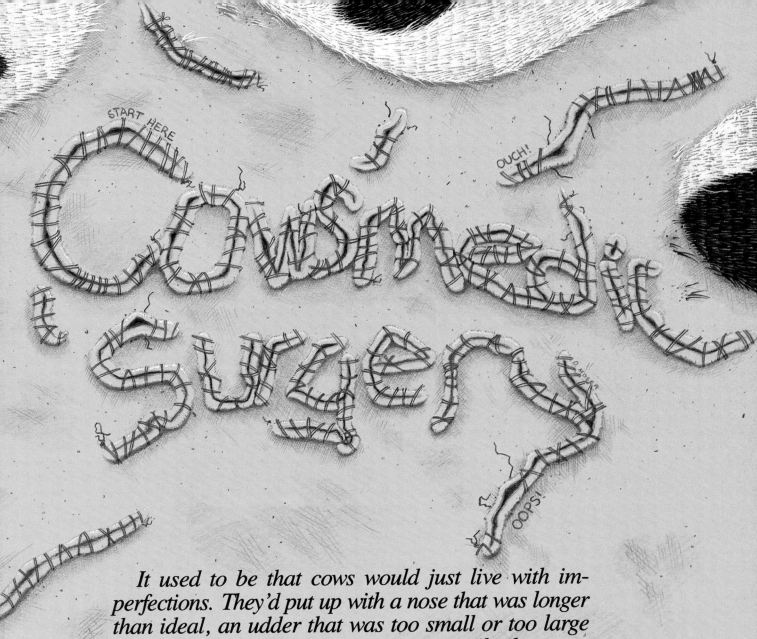

Cowsmedic Surgery

It used to be that cows would just live with imperfections. They'd put up with a nose that was longer than ideal, an udder that was too small or too large (by national standards) or a gummy smile that was, well, gummy.

Times have changed. Cows no longer have to live with the shame or with the fear that their lovers will one day leave them for a luxury model because of their lack or overabundance of certain physical attributes.

This issue of Cowsmo explores the world of cowsmedic surgery. It reveals how four simple operations can change the way you live, for better or for worse, from richer to poorer. (You may now kiss the groom — and your money — goodbye.)

Correcting that gummy smile

Do you hold back big smiles so as not to reveal too much gum? Do you cover your mouth with one or both hoofs when you break into laughter?

If gummy smile is something you've always hated about yourself, learn how simple plastic surgery, the insertion of a piece of plastic under your lip, can end this hatred. Sounds romantic? It is. That's right, girls, the answer to your problem is right under your nose and you didn't even know it! What are you waiting for?

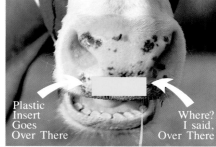

Plastic Insert Goes Over There

Where? I said, Over There

▲ BEFORE

Gummy smile is a result of short elevator muscles These muscles are responsible for lifting your upper lip above the gum line, thus having the undesirable effect of exposing your wretched gums for others to view.

▲ AFTER

Twelve weeks after the operation, the implant is firmly in place, stitches have been removed and the healing process is now complete. You now have a perfect smile with no gumminess present to annoy friends and associates. Chances of the plastic insertion abcessing are slim.

Gummy Smile Corrective Procedure

Location of the plastic implant is marked on upper lip. Muscles are sliced down the middle, like one might slice a kaiser roll. The implant is then slid in between the severed muscles not unlike how one might insert a piece of ham or other favorite luncheon meat (preferably pork, chicken or lamb) between the above-mentioned kaiser roll.

A local anesthetic is used. This is the type of anesthesia where the physician can't play touchy-feely with you (without you knowing it) while you are unconscious — because you aren't unconscious. This is the kind of anesthesia you want . . . Or is it?

Benefits:	. . . . .No more gummy smile (if it's a success).
Cost:	. . . .$2400
Operation Time:	. . . . .Two hours
Healing Time:	. . . . . . .Twelve weeks
Drawbacks:	. . ."Hey! What did you do to your lip?"

Nose Reduction

The Nose Job™ is a simple but pricey operation which involves the breaking of the nose presently renting or leasing space on your face. Commonly referred to as, "your nose" or "that thing".

The surgeon then sculpts a new, smaller nose, conveniently right on your face. There is no waiting. No long, drawn-out ordeal like when you send Kodachrome away to Kodak for processing these days.

Patient usually experiences two black eyes as the result of fracturing the nose.

▲ BEFORE

Benefits:	. .No more "Liar, liar, pants on fire, nose is as long as a telephone wire."
Cost:	. . . .$5000
Operation Time:	. . . . .Five hours
Healing Time:	. . . . .Four weeks
Drawbacks:	. . . . .No more 5000 bucks!

◀ AFTER

Bonehead Condition

Bonehead condition occurs as a result of a rampant growth on the top of the headbone. It usually happens during youth when the likelihood of, say, an original idea or something equally as exciting is more apt to take place. This, coupled with sudden, frantic bursts of optimism, makes the brain think that it will have to expand. The headbone grows rapidly to make room for the enlarged brain — but the brain does not grow.

In fact, it doesn't do anything. It just sits there with an "I'm in control" sign pinned to its forehead. Something happened. It's known

as adulthood. As the size of the pay check increases, the number of original ideas decreases. After marriage, the brain becomes even smaller. However, the headbone, or "bonehead", as it will soon be called, does not decrease in size. Consequently, the extra space does not go away. It's like an attic apartment. You can either take in a student or close it up.

In cows where extra height is not necessary and/or where headbanging is already a problem, a simple operation to reduce height by removing 3–5 inches of headbone seems attractive.

Bonehead Corrective Procedure

This simple operation entails the lancing of the hide from ear to ear, taking the over-the-top-of-the-head route. The instrument used in the lancing process is a very, very sharp scalpel. (The kind crazed lunatics carry in their front pockets. They believe, in their own twisted way, that they are, indeed, providing a service to the general public, or at least to anyone who glances at them sideways. Better known as the wrong way!)

After the incision is made, a high-speed bone saw is used to, simply, remove un-needed bone. The excess hide is removed and the incision is sewn back up again. C'est tu!

The whole operation is, of course, performed by a qualified physician. Not by a hack, as stated in the newspapers last week.

Benefits:	No more "Hey Bonehead!"
Cost:	$3000
Operation Time:	Two hours
Healing Time:	Four to six weeks
Drawbacks:	No more "Hey Bonehead!" Now nobody says anything.

Udder Enlargement

Otherwise known as the "Hey baby! Baboomba! Baboomba! Holy Mackerel, Andy! Look out, Ma, they're comin' to get me! I just died and went to heaven! Why are you hanging around with that goof, anyway? Let's go to Vegas and spend my nest egg! Nest egg? What nest egg? That's not a nest egg! There's plenty more where that came from! You called me all the way out here to tell me that the photo copier was broken? . . . Well, well, stutter, stutter, trip, fumble, shake, jitter, Lord help me, Miss Prism . . . Let's see if I can fix it for you! Eerrrrrt! Watch where the hell you're driving! Tell me about it, Ned! . . . Didn't you see what was standing on all glorious fours back there at that last corner?" operation.

Because it's "otherwise-known-as" name is a bit lengthy, it's better known as "Udder Enlargement".

We aren't going to tell you how this operation is done. However, we will say that it is as simple as blowing up an air mattress. And it's as costly as anything can be when you want something which you don't have, and you're prepared to pay anything to get it.

◀ BEFORE

AFTER ▼

Benefits:	Carefully read Udder Enlargement, "otherwise known as the . . ."
Cost:	Who cares!
Operation Time:	Six hours
Healing Time:	Four weeks
Drawbacks:	Carefully read Udder Enlargement, "otherwise known as the . . ."

Romance Excerpt

THE CONTINUING SAGA OF CHUCK AND DI

Sensational steak, fabulous fries, wonderful garnish, and then something went horribly wrong…

Chuck sat in the chair by the window, his plate gleaming in the dazzling afternoon sunshine. Diana paced the floor, collecting herself. An hour passed before she could muster up the courage to speak.

"Face it, Chuck, you're a steak!" She shook her head in disgust. Diana could not believe what her eyes were seeing.

"I'm a steak? An hour of pacing and that's all you can say? What's the matter, don't you like the cut? Remember, you're the one who said I had to change or it was over."

"The cut's fine, Chuck. A bit chewy, perhaps, but fine. It's just not what I was expecting. A haircut I could handle—even a tattoo—but this is bizarre. It's . . . it's . . . it's so extreme that I'm very, very upset."

"Yes, I can see that. You don't normally say 'it's' three times in a row unless there's something horribly wrong. What exactly is it about my new 'do' that upsets you? The fries? The garnish? Say the word and I'll get rid of them."

"You know I hate fries. And frankly, I've never been fussy about garnish. Nobody eats it, Chuck. It's a bloody waste!"

"Fries? What fries? They're cold, anyway. Here, have a bite. I was sitting under a heat lamp for ten minutes waiting for someone to finish their salad. Not my idea of a good time. I got tired of waiting so I thought I'd sort of stroll over here and surprise you."

"Well, you did a good job in the surprise department, Chuck."

"Oh, come off it! What's the big deal about fries and garnish, anyway?"

"It's not just fries and garnish. There's a bit of a size problem here."

"That's no different than before . . . There's not a hell of a lot I can do about that . . ."

"I'm not referring to *that,* Chuck. My point is quite clear. I'm 1200 pounds and you're 15¾ ounces. Your stunt, Chuck, has made a simple, enjoyable, romantic drive in the country an impossibility."

"We could still go on a picnic. You could drive, I won't mind."

"Chuck! You *are* a picnic! I hate to crush you, but I'm afraid it's over."

"But! . . . But! . . . But! . . ."

"No 'Buts', Chuck. There isn't time. Remember, this is an excerpt."

"Lookit! We can sort this out before we get to the bottom of the page!"

"And who's going to buy the book if we do, huh, Chuck? Who's going to buy it? Get a grip on your life, Chuck! We're living in a world of sequels."

"Just say you'll try! Say it now!"

"Chuck, the bottom of the page is the bottom of the page. Changing the type size isn't going to change the outcome."

"You noticed! You do love me after all!"

"I'll need time."

"How much time? A word? A sentence? A paragraph? Please don't say longer than a paragraph!"

"I'm not going to give you false hopes, Chuck. It could be longer than a paragraph. It might be a chapter . . ."

"A CHAPTER!!! I'll kill myself before I last a chapter! I just know it . . ."

"You've wasted a paragraph already, Chuck. Why don't we drop the subject and save something for the book?"

"Okay! But I'll need an answer . . . Soon! . . . All right?!? No tricks, okay?"

The Maidenfarm Cow...
Never knows where she's going.

She creates her own itinerary
and lets Chanteaty®
create the rest.
All canvas, cotton, and
sophistication...
In a world of confusion,
the Maidenfarm® cow
wanders all on her own.

What has four legs,
looks great,
and loves to be
worn out?

Hint: (Besides your lover)

COURT FINDS COW INNOCENT IN P.M.S. SLAYING OF HUSBAND

LONDON (REUTERS): They said it couldn't happen. Then they said it was improbable. Then they said it was inevitable. Now they tell us that the inevitable is a reality. Who are "they"? Why do "they" change their minds so much?

An eleven year old Holstein from Brighton is one lucky cow today, as twelve jurors (six cows, three horses, two chickens and a duck thrown in for good measure) handed down the "not guilty" verdict. It certainly was a day for firsts. The *first* time Treena Wildfong had ever been charged with the *first* degree murder of her *first* and only husband, the late Mr. Edward (Skip) Wildfong I. She is a barnwife, he was an artificial insemination technician.

This wasn't just an ordinary murder trial, though. When the "not guilty" verdict was read aloud, the former Mrs. Edward

(Skip) Wildfong made history. She was also very relieved.

You see, Treena Wildfong had pleaded "not guilty by reason of premenstrual stress (PMS)", sometimes referred to by sufferers of the syndrome as "temporary insanity" (I'll kill you. I haven't figured out how, yet, but I'll find a way. Then we'll see who's dead and who isn't.).

A jammed courtroom, with representatives from all the areas of agriculture, listened in horror as Mrs. Wildfong relived the nightmare. She spoke of how she snuck up behind Ed's chair, then asked him to guess what it was she was going to do. He was watching "Wild World of Sports", his eyes glued to the T.V.

"His first three guesses were stupid. It was obvious to me that he wasn't the slightest bit interested in our little game. 'You're going to

bake a pie, Treena.' 'You're going to polish some silverware, Treena.' 'You're going to work on one of your many little projects, Treena.' "

"I honestly didn't mean to kill him. If Ed had said, 'You're going to bludgeon me to death with a frigging rolling pin, Treena.' 'What the hell has come over you, Treena?' 'Have you gone completely mad, Treena?', I probably wouldn't have done it."

WHEN I FEEL GOOD, I FEEL VERY, VERY GOOD BUT WHEN I FEEL BAD I'M A BITCH

"Okay! Okay! So I admit I was a bitch but it's not going to bring Ed back. He didn't even get to see the end of the show. He'll never watch 'Wild World of Sports' ever again. He'll never artificially inseminate another cow as long as he lives. And that, need I remind you, is not

A rather subdued (showing no glee at all) Treena Wildfong leaves court a free cow.

a very long time. He would have to be awfully quick. Fast Eddie or no Fast Eddie, it's almost impossible."

"It's not even like we were fighting over the cable television converter, as was often the case. I mean, that would have been reason enough."

"I was baking a pie when the feeling struck. I stopped and looked into the living room. The image that I saw wasn't harsh. It was just Ed. He was plunked down in front of the television watching his favorite

see **Ed's Dead**, Page 2

AGRI-PHOBIA —
THE CRIPPLING FEAR OF AGRICULTURE

"Nooooooo! Pleeeeease! Don't make me go out in the fieeeeld!"

"But I don't waaaant to drink from the water trough outsiiiiide. That's why I have a water bowl in heeere!"

Call it silly, call it pathetic, but this is what the day-to-day is like for millions of cows around the world.

The syndrome is called "Agriphobia" (fear of agriculture, we think). But it's not just the cultivation of crops that these cows fear. It seems to be everything. It seems to be deeper than this. The cause, unknown. The cure, an unsolved mystery.

Some medical experts speculate that sufferers have a silly notion that one day they'll be lured into a truck, taken to the bus station and sent off, free of charge, on a three-week excursion package tour of central Canada.

What is it about Canada that these cows fear most? The climate? The Canadian people themselves (individually)? The Canadian people, en masse? Are they secretly afraid that they will have a chance

meeting with someone who works for the Canadian Broadcasting Corporation (C.B.C.)? Someone who has been researching a story for the past six months. A story which will cost a fortune to produce, will reach the stage of "in the can" but will, most likely, never be aired.

Others scoff at this theory. Still others scoff at the suggestion that it is, in fact, a theory at all. They feel that it's purely speculation, as is clearly stated not more than two paragraphs ago. They also feel that these "others" who scoffed are even sillier than the agriphobics because the word "theory" wasn't mentioned until they opened their big traps (and out it came).

However, "others" and "still others" do agree that the syndrome has little to do with Canada or the C.B.C. (Canadian Broadcasting Corporation). Some feel that their fears span from fence posts all the way up to (and including) the music of Barry Manilow. What is it about fence posts and, for that matter, Barry Manilow, that these cows fear?

Is it his current hit (if he has one) or is it his sketchy advertising-jingle past? Was it his smash hit, "You deserve a steak today at McDonald's?" But if they (McDonald's) really and truly "Do it all for ewe", shouldn't it be sheep instead of cows who indirectly fear Barry Manilow?

Such are the mysteries of this peculiar syndrome. Such are the mysteries of these ordinary, every-day cows who could be mistaken for you and me.

Does the fact that no agriphobic has ever visited Salt Lake City, Utah, tell us anything? What is it about Mormons that terrifies these

INSIDE THE MOOS

Pig trouble worsens — Take-over inevitable

Proconfusionists — They want "whatever", and they want it NOW!

Insight: Where do we "GO" from here?

YOUR MORNING SMILE

All women become like their mothers. That is their tragedy. No man does. That's his.

— Oscar Wilde —

cows? They love salt, so it couldn't be Salt Lake City itself or the state of Utah. So that just leaves the Mormons. Is it the Mormon Tabernacle choir? Their incredible wealth? Their bigamistic past? The bizarre hold that they have over their followers? A bizarre hold which spans from fence posts (the "everyday Joe" Mormons) all the way up to (and including) The Osmonds®. And what have "they" done musically, lately?

Do cows secretly fear domination by Mormons? Why would Mormons want to dominate cows? They have their fingers in enough pies already. Even if there were a market for "cow pies", is this an area of business they would want to expand into? I think not.

Perhaps it's none of the above. Perhaps it's the twenty-first century that they fear. Or just the fear of fear itself.

Contented they are to remain indoors. Away from the great outdoors. Away from agriculture, away from the twenty-first century. Away! Away! You please me not.

If it is, in fact, the fear of fear, then "these cows" are not going to go very far. And that suits "these cows" just fine.

Indeed, such are the mysteries of this peculiar and crippling syndrome.

PROCONFUSIONIST GROUP TO HOLD RALLY ON ABORTION QUESTION NEXT TUESDAY OR WEDNESDAY AT THE LATEST (MAYBE)

Make way for the Proconfusionists. They're the newest group in the abortion rights question and, for all they know, they may even be hopping mad.

The pro-abortion group accuses them of being wishy-washy. The anti-abortionists think that they're fence sitters. The pro-choice group feels that they are a bunch of disorganized idiots (but quickly add, "But that's entirely up to them.").

BROUGHT TOGETHER BY FATE

Nobody is really sure where the Proconfusionists came from. Rumor has it that they simply stopped what they were doing and formed a crowd. Unlike other groups, where one cow is usually the driving force and the rest follow along behind, the Proconfusionists have no one at the helm.

As one member puts it, "Having nobody running 'The Organization' (and I use these words loosely) only confuses the issue and that's the way we like to keep it. Nice and tidy!"

Their first meeting was a rather unique experience. Brought together perhaps by fate, without quite knowing the reasons why, they became one big quagulating mass of confusion. They began chanting, "Whatever, now! Whatever, now! Whatever, now!". At least until somebody yelled out of an upstairs window (a la Bugs Bunny), "NEAAAA! SHAD AAAAP!"

A hush fell over the crowd. For a second, some feared that they might stop quagulating. For a split second, they all feared that they might become organized. Then came the second assault from the same upstairs window, "NEAAAA! WHAT A BUNCH OF MAROONS!"

The hush was much louder now and it seemed like they might even be gaining momentum. And then, without warning, they retaliated as a group: "NEAAAA! SHAD AAAP! YOURSELF!"; followed by the lethal blow of "SO LONG SCREWY, SEE YA IN ST. LEWIE!". Divided they stood. The Proconfusionist group was born.

SO WHAT ARE THE ISSUES?

The issues are precisely what they don't intend to find out at the next meeting. That is, if they manage to succeed in having a next meeting. They are aware of the realities of their situation. They're caught up in a Catch-22. You can't have a meeting without issues but without a meeting, you won't know what the issues are. Well, maybe a Catch-20 or 21. It's right up there in that area of the low "Catch-Twenties", that's for sure. Ain't no doubt about it, they're caught up in something that has a catchy name and they don't like it one little bit.

THE CURE A MYSTERY, THE CAUSE UNKNOWN

The Proconfusionists are not stupid. Neither are they rebels without a cause. They are rebels; this they know. The cause? Well, it appears as though someone has either misplaced it _or_ it hasn't come in on the truck yet.

Not unlike other groups, the Proconfusionists aren't sure if there is a solution to the abortion question. A better understanding of what the abortion question _is_ might provide some answers. If the answers happen to appear of their own free will, then it's fine and dandy with them. But the Proconfusionists are not about to upset any apple carts to go looking for them.

SO WHAT ABOUT THE BIG QUESTION?

As far as the "Big Question" (when are they having their next meeting?) goes, many soon-to-be-members think next Tuesday would be a nice day. Wednesday at the latest (maybe). But a handful of purists believe that it should, again, just happen and to organize one would be sacrilegious. Almost every other will-be-member expressed a deep concern about giving away party secrets and felt that they weren't prepared to comment at the time because this sort of thing would naturally be discussed at the next meeting. Then and only then would they be prepared to spill the beans. "But thanks, anyway," they said.

Such are the mysteries of the Proconfusionist group.

They simply stopped what they were doing and formed a crowd.

Ed's Dead

program, his belt beginning to show strain from the beer gut he's been working on. Ed's project. Ya! Ed had a gut. Lots of guys his age do. Do I kill him for that? No, I wouldn't think so."

"But then this thought popped into my head. This quiet little voice that said, 'You _know_'. (It gave the word "know" special emphasis.) Ed would probably just as soon die as not get to watch 'Wild World of Sports'. And that was it. I didn't have to look around for a murder weapon. I was already holding the rolling pin as best I could. It was BONK and down Ed went as effortlessly as the middle of a cake when you open the oven door before its time. Ed was the worst for that. I'd say, 'Ed! Don't open that oven door! I've got a cake in there, damn it! A cake, Ed! You know what a cake is, don't ya, Ed?' ".

"I mean, in a sense Ed was right. I _was_ baking a pie. If he'd have guessed that five minutes earlier, it might not have happened. His life was in his own hoofs and he didn't even know it. But I'll tell ya, had it been baseball trivia he'd have been sittin' up rhyming off the answers left and right and waving his front legs like a madman."

THEN, FOR A MOMENT, ALL EYES WERE ON THE DUCK

Treena Wildfong stopped talking for a moment. She had tolerated the duck long enough. She had tried to pretend that it had not been sticking the tips of its wings in its ears (if you could call them ears) while she had been trying to talk. She hoped that it would stop making the duck noises around the courtroom after a few good "Rak! Rak! Rak!"s. But it was not to be.

He had been zeroing in on minority groups, mostly sheep and goats. You want to hear a sheep bleat? Give it a weird look and go "Rak! Rak! Rak!" in its face in a public situation where a reserved conduct code is required.

The judge hadn't said anything. It was, after all, the _first_ time a duck had had this type of official duty bestowed upon it. The judge didn't want to publicly embarrass the duck and, in a sense, all ducks. Those present in the courtroom and, of course, those back in the barn watching the trial on television. His Honor had fully intended to take him aside during recess for some crash lessons in court procedure. Unfortunately, the accused took it upon herself to spare His Honor the bother.

Treena Wildfong was not about to let the duck get away with anything. In her mind, court was not an ideal setting for improv. This was not a comedy cabaret. It was her day in court and she's already heard six more Rak! Rak! Rak!s than she cared to hear today.

A strange look passed over her. Her tail began switching. Beads of sweat were noticeable on her forehead. She addressed the Judge.

"Maybe, Your Honor, if the duck insists on making faces and rude noises . . . just maybe it would like to step out in the lobby and I could demonstrate how I make pie over at my place. Would the duck enjoy a few seconds of home economics instruction? Hmm?"

The duck slunched down in his seat. He was trying to look as much unlike a duck as possible. It wasn't working. There wasn't one question he could think of, off the top of his head, that he cared to ask Treena Wildfong in the area of home economics. Besides, he suspected her of having an excellent recipe for duck soup. There was no question now that the Rak! Rak! Rak!s had been a horrible mistake. A mistake that he would have to live down. The duck world holds no place for wise guys. He had already resigned himself to the fact that it was not going to be an overnight comeback.

With the quacker well in his place, Treena Wildfong went on to finish her gruesome story. And in the end, she did manage to win the sympathy of the jury, including Mr. Facemaker, the court jester.

And when she stopped talking, you could have heard a pin drop in that courtroom. But did anybody drop one? No! They had all been too busy listening. They just sat there in shock; cows, pigs, horses, chickens and ducks. All of them. And all of them were thanking their lucky stars that their name wasn't Edward (Skip) Wildfong. And if they ever _had_ wanted to be "The Skipper", it certainly wasn't today.

PIGS TO ATTEMPT ANOTHER WORLD TAKEOVER NEXT WEEK

Spokespig

Those tricky pigs are at it again. Only this time, it's the world (Hardy! Har! Har!).

A spokespig for the Pig Infiltration Group (P.I.G.) said, "If you thought that 'Chicken Man' was everywhere (He's everywhere! He's everywhere!), then you're in for a 'pig surprise'. Let me just say that compared to what's going to happen next week, 'Chicken Man' (He's everywhere! He's every-where!) was absolutely nowhere — and I might add, without a beak.

"There are a lot of us and we're all sick and tired of getting the short end of the stick. Pigs have been confined to the less-than-glamorous areas of the barn. It's high time our concerns became your concerns. If it takes taking over the world and placing the ~~foo on the other shoot shot shit~~ shoe on the other foot to prove our points then I guess that's what it takes."

BAN ON KABOBS TOP PRIORITY FOR PIGS

Pigs claim that the first thing to go after next week's takeover will be "kabobs". This isn't too radical as it should benefit cows as well as other animals which are, shall we say, "kabobbable". The pigs are also thinking about broadening the ban to cover other atrocities such as "Nuggets". As yet, cows and pigs are not likely candidates for "Nuggets", but that's not to say that they are not "Nuggetable".

Poultry (particularly chickens) should experience GLEE when they hear this little bit of news (that is, if chickens experience anything at all). There will also be an immediate inquiry into the practise of breading.

Any products involving domestic animals which are, to quote a frightening advertisement, "Crunchy, golden brown on the outside, tender, juicy and delicious on the inside" will be under severe scrutiny.

Pigs are also lobbying heavily for the removal of the words "Hardy! Har! Har!" from the beginning of this very article.

"Slim chance of that," said a cow. "This sucker's already gone to press!"

"Well, if that's the case," replied a pig, "Then Hardy! Hardy! Hardy! Har! Har! to you, and we'll see you next week."

P.M.P. Has Arrived
Government Introduces Premenstrual Pension Plan

STOP COMPLAINING AND START LIVING

We've seen what P.M.S. can do. It has been responsible for trouble on the homefront, tension in the office and at least one accidental death (bonking) in Brighton. Perhaps all of this will soon come to an abrupt end as did the life of Edward (Skip) Wildfong. But let's not get into that again.

The Government believes that while some medications do help ease some of the symptoms of P.M.S., they feel that nothing is going to eradicate the problem of the Syndrome quite like their Premenstrual Pension Plan, which was unveiled today on Capital Hill.

The recipients of the P.M.P. benefit will be those who suffer from extreme tension prior to "that time".

There is, however, one small hitch. They (the recipients) will have to be pleasant (for a change) to everyone from now on. No more tantrums. No more "Eat it and shut up"s. No more "You're going to get a damn good licking when we get home"s. No more "You're really gunning for it aren't you, Harry"s.

For many, it will be a difficult challenge. For many, it will be impossible.

YOU TOO CAN TURN THAT SNARKY PERSONALITY INTO CASH

How do I qualify?

* You must be truly bitchy.
* You must have three other cows (family, coworkers, former friends) to attest to the fact that you are indeed bitchy.
* You must be able to swear a blue streak at, and in the presence of, a benefit officer.
* You must respond favorably when asked the following questions:

1) Do you mind if I have a bunch of the boys over tonight to lounge around and watch the game? And, oh yes, do you think you could slap together some sandwich trays — we're bound to get a little hungry?

2) Would you type this letter over for me during the lunch hour?

3) Can Christine sleep over tonight, Mom?

4) Would you pass the butter please, Honey?

5) Could you do me a little favor?

6) Your hair looks different, Honey Bun. What on earth did you do to it?

Those who qualify will have one hundred dollars per month placed in a pension plan for them. They will not be able to draw from it until they reach age sixty-five. (Well after meadowpause).

ABUSE OF THE SYSTEM

The government recognizes that "Where there is a will there is a way", but recipients will still have to fall within the guidelines which have been laid down. They still have to pass the test. However they admit that there still could be some trouble from one particular group. The I.W.T.T.F.O.T.H.A.T.D.O.A.-H.A.A.A.A.B.A. (Individuals Who Tend To Fly Off The Handle At The Drop Of A Hat And Are Almost Always Bitchy Anyway). This is one bunch of cows that we're going to be on the lookout for.

We still don't think that they (I.W.T.T.F.O.T.H.A.T.D.O.A.H.-A.A.A.A.B.A.) are going to be a problem because one hundred dollars a month is not going to be a big enough perk to keep them from lashing out. I mean, we are asking a lot! They are just not the kind of cows you can say, "Here's a hundred bucks a month, now shut up for thirty years, would ya?" to.

INSIGHT
Where Do We "Go" From Here?

It used to be you'd "go" wherever and whenever you pleased. You simply never asked. You didn't have to. Numero uno et numero deux, aussi. That's the way it was. Those haydays have come and gone.

Was it waste? Extravagance? Carelessness?

Waste? For sure. Extravagance? Maybe. Carelessness? Never! It was intentional. It was fun. And you didn't even have to clean it up. Somebody else did . . . or it just seemed to get magically carried away. But not anymore.

Today, elderly cattle shake their heads, as do the younger ones who choose to stand alongside them. Because today, here, on this farm, through no fault of their own, the flies are particularly bad.

Nancy, a cow of considerable years, a feminist, a life-long member and co-founder of "Waste Not", an organization which has been fighting careless waste since 1962, admits, "There'll always be waste. But I'm a firm believer of everything in its rightful place."

"I recall days," said Nancy, "When it was commonplace to hear somebody yell from the other end of the meadow (as if we cared) 'Hey, everybody! Look! Over here! Wanna watch me spell my name?'. Smartasses.

"There were even teams. Agribatics, they called it. They dive-bombed everyone. Gangs was closer to the truth! 'The Brown Angels', 'Johnny P. Good and the Yellow Jackets' and so on. They were deranged, but even that didn't seem to stop them."

"It isn't fair for the young ones coming on. History is full of it, though. Generations dumping their problems on future generations. And in the name of fertilizer! Into the laps of babes doth go this fertilizer. Doeth we thinketh twice of what we seemeth to be readily prepared to do to our children and to our children's children and to our children's children's children? Do we thinketh once? I thinketh not. But I thinketh, as (Thank God) doeth others."

If there be an answer, pray tell: Where does it lie?

In the pasture, my friend, in the pasture.

REVLOIN

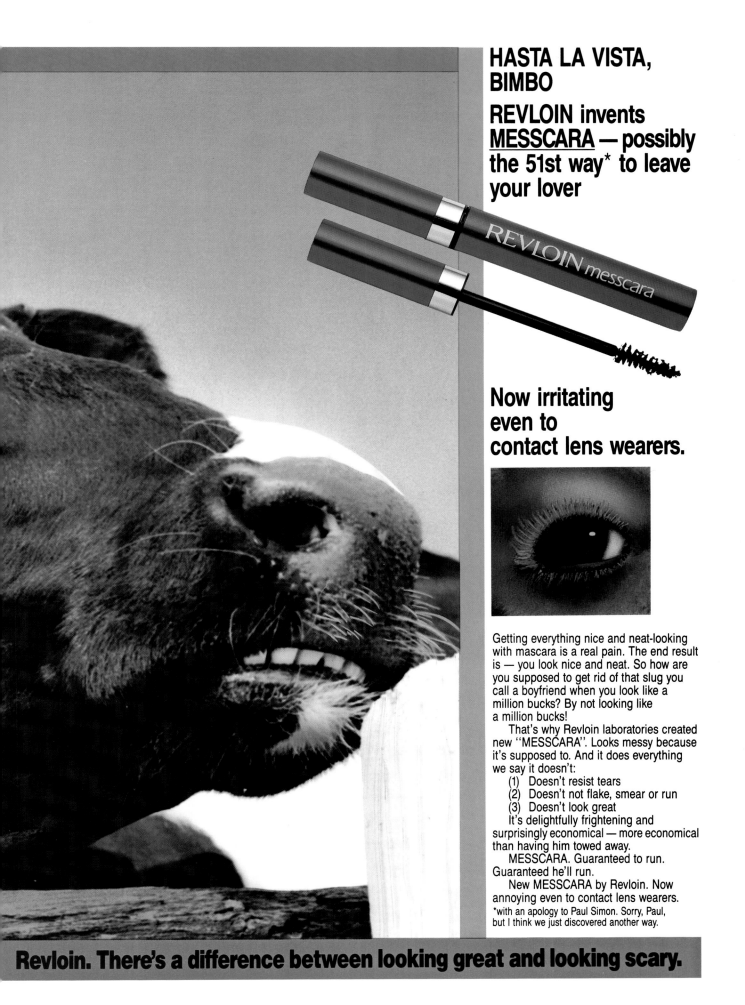

HASTA LA VISTA, BIMBO

REVLOIN invents MESSCARA — possibly the 51st way* to leave your lover

Now irritating even to contact lens wearers.

Getting everything nice and neat-looking with mascara is a real pain. The end result is — you look nice and neat. So how are you supposed to get rid of that slug you call a boyfriend when you look like a million bucks? By not looking like a million bucks!

That's why Revloin laboratories created new "MESSCARA". Looks messy because it's supposed to. And it does everything we say it doesn't:

(1) Doesn't resist tears
(2) Doesn't not flake, smear or run
(3) Doesn't look great

It's delightfully frightening and surprisingly economical — more economical than having him towed away.

MESSCARA. Guaranteed to run. Guaranteed he'll run.

New MESSCARA by Revloin. Now annoying even to contact lens wearers.

*with an apology to Paul Simon. Sorry, Paul, but I think we just discovered another way.

Revloin. There's a difference between looking great and looking scary.

cowsmo all sells

❶ COWSMO FRONT COVER
The original COWSMOPOLITAN front cover in full color with all of the hilarious text.

YOU'VE READ THE BOOK ...NOW GET THE SHIRTS!

Let's get one thing straight! We're not trying to fool anyone. We realize, as much as the next person, that merchandizing *is* the "Devil's Handiwork". But we also believe that you shouldn't leave the house without a clean, funny shirt on, just in case you're hospitalized. Popularity has never been easier to attain. Yes, "boisterous gaiety" anxiously awaits you moments after slipping into one or all of the COWSMO COLLECTORS T's and Sweats. All sweats and T's are made from (quality) 100% cotton (white only), and decorated with the full color graphics which helped make COWSMOPOLITAN a best seller. So what is it? The Devil's Handiwork or hilarious quality at the right price? We think it's the latter. We think you'll agree. Order now!

❷ The **MR. AVAIL. A. BULL** centerfold shirt in full color ("Something in the way you moove me".) For him or her.

❹ HOLSTEIN DIOR, from YAK'S FIFTH AVENUE — High fashion for him or her.

❸ "THE GIRLS JUST WANNA HAVE FUN" — Life in the "Back lane" will never be the same! For him or her, in full color.

POSTCARD

MOO YORK, MOO YORK, U.S.A.
4/9/87
POSTAL SERVICE

Dear Elsie
Remember when we used to have to hide behind the barn to sneak a smoke? Times sure have changed. Now we can vote, have affairs, and light up a buff anytime we choose, just like bulls. Anyway, I'm delighted to hear you're in calf. Make sure you smoke plenty of cigarettes during pregnancy, I read somewhere it's really good for the baby. Take care,
Love Molly

P.S. Could you send me some matches? I got mine taken away!

TO=
Elsie(the)Cow
Stall #26.
The Barn
U.S.A.

VIRGINIA SKIMS
You've come a long way, Maybe.

SURGEON GENERAL'S WARNING: Smoking during pregnancy is stupid! Molly's full of cowplop! Don't send her any matches either. Take care.
Love Surgio

Also Available in 2% and Homogenized.

COWSMOPOLITAN
™

◄ **MOOING YOUR FOOL HEAD OFF ALL OVER THE MEADOW AS IF THAT'S GOING TO CHANGE ANYTHING.** Does it help? (A Quiz).

ROMANCE EXCERPT: "SURPRISE! SURPRISE! SURPRISE!" The "other cow" was my lover's sister. Which means my husband's son was *my* nephew. Find out the rest of the dirt next month, when "Incest" visits Cowsmo.

INTERVIEW (sort of): "YOU DON'T HAVE TO BE PLASTIC BUT IT HELPS!" Cowsmo talks ► to a model BUT the model does not talk to Cowsmo. What's it like to be a top model? How much money do they make? Are models stuck up? Do they really like to date wimpy bulls? What do they do for excitement when it seems like they've done it all already? Do they secretly fear putting on the beef when they stop modeling? THESE questions and more will remain a mystery, next month, when COWSMO talks to a model.

◄ **WHAT'S THAT HANGING FROM YOUR NOSE?** (A Quiz). Sometimes you're so close to things that are dangling from your nose that you can't tell what they are. Sound all too familiar? Find out what it is next month. And remember, don't blow your nose in the meantime — that's cheating.

FEMININE INCHING: WHAT HAPPENS WHEN YOU'RE CRAWLING ALONG THE . . . PARDON?!? OH! . . . Feminine itching . . . Oh, no, no, no. We don't have anything on that. I'm sorry, can't help you out there. Just inching. Lookit! Go ahead and cancel the article . . . Just see if I care!

ARE TWO HEADS BETTER THAN NONE? Next month you'll meet Helga and Heidi. ► They shared the same body but not the same philosophies. They shared the same hay fever but not the same boyfriends. One liked classical music but was afraid of heights; the other loved skydiving and was very, very good at it. What happens when they both decide to leave?

◄ **THOSE FABULOUS OUT-TAKES FROM THE KOWLUA SHOOT.** What happens when "This Stupid Horse Can Be Yours" and a drunken bottle of "Oil of Old Hay" barge into the studio and onto the set of the Kowlua shoot? In a word, chaos. You won't want to miss any of it! Catch the excitement, the photos, the interviews. Meet the photographer and those sexy creative types when Cowsmo visits the photo studio where all hell broke loose.

AFTER YOU'VE PUSHED "MR. EASILY MANIPULATED" INTO MARRIAGE . . . THEN WHAT? Find out what to do with your little cream puff now that you've finally got him.

THE PROBLEM OF LEG SUCKING — Walk through any field. Stroll through any barn. ► It's there. Leg sucking. And, it's more popular than ever before. A serious side effect of Leg Sucking, is Leg Fetish. The worship of legs. And although there's nothing quite like a nice set of legs, many psychiatrists feel that there is no point in getting weird about it. Find out all about this puzzling problem, next month, in COWSMO.

— PLUS TONS OF ADS AGAIN AND MULCH, MULCH MORE —